Contents

Age-Appropriate Skills

Language

- following directions
- story comprehension
- descriptive and comparative language
- rhyming
- categorization
- letter and sound recognition
- statements and questions
- auditory and visual memory
- left to right tracking
- oral language
- vocabulary and concept development
- sequencing
- color words

Math

- counting to 20
- patterning
- numeral recognition
- geometric shapes
- ordinal numbers
- beginning computation
- one-to-one matching
- graphing
- measurement

Circle-Time Books

 Making Circle-Time Books ....

Follow these simple directions to assemble a circle-time book for each of the five sections of *The Ocean*.

- Tear out and laminate the color story pages for each circle-time book.

- Bind the books with binder rings or an alternative binding method.

- Read the circle-time book as the opening activity for each section of *The Ocean*.

Place the book on an easel or chalkboard stand and flip the pages for easy reading.

 Sharing Circle-Time Books ....

Each circle-time story introduces the topic of that section. Begin by reading the story to the children several times. The first time you read it, you might ask children to predict what the story will be about by looking at the cover illustration. In subsequent readings, use strategies such as:

- moving your finger under words as you read to model left to right tracking

- allowing children to "read" the predictable text

- asking children to identify objects in the pictures

- talking about any rhyming words

- asking children to predict what will happen next in the story

- asking questions to help children recall story details

- asking at least one question that relates to children's own lives

Circle-Time Books

"Maggie's Trip to the Ocean" (pages 13–22)
Use this colorful book to introduce children to the ocean. Pause on each page to discuss the illustrations. Point to each plant, animal, and ocean feature shown in the illustration. Discuss what Maggie is wearing to explore each area of the ocean. Explain that *ocean* and *sea* both name the same place in this story. Let children share what they know about the ocean from their own experiences.

Ask questions such as:

- What do you think Maggie will see at the ocean?

- What did she see when she looked in the (tide pool, kelp forest, deep ocean)?

- How did Maggie look at the (kelp forest, deep ocean)?

- If you lived near the ocean, what would you like to see?

Section Two
Near the Shore

"1, 2, 3 What Do You See?" (pages 51–60)
This book introduces plants and animals that live along the shore, in tide pools, and in the kelp forest. Use the illustrations to name the plants and animals. For example:

- Kelp in the kelp forest grows as tall as trees.

- Anemones look like flowers, but they are animals.

- Barnacles wave their tentacles to pull food out of the water.

Ask questions such as:

- What animal do you see here? What is it doing?

- How many (name animal) do you see? How is the animal moving?

- Can you name another animal that (swims, waves its arms, etc.)?

Section Three
In the Deep Ocean

"I Live in the Ocean" (pages 87–96)
This story introduces animals that live in the open ocean. Use this story as an opportunity to build concepts about the various animals.

- A whale is not a fish. It must come to the surface to breathe air.

- Sea turtles are very large turtles. They come ashore to lay their eggs.

- Many fish swim in groups called schools. This helps keep them safe.

Ask questions such as:

- Can you name this animal?

- How does the animal move in the ocean?

- Which animals have soft bodies?

- Ocean animals move in different ways. What ways can you move?

Circle-Time Books

"Sailing, Sailing" (pages 129–138)
This funny story contains a simple rhyme about sea creatures watching people moving on or through the water in different kinds of vehicles.

Ask questions such as:

- What did the (hermit crab, sea lion, etc.) see?
- Who knows a word that names the kind of sea boat that needs paddles to make it move?
- What two words sound the same on each page of this story?
- Have you ever taken a boat ride? Tell about your ride.

"Clean It Up!" (pages 163–172)
In this story, a family is upset by the mess they find at their favorite beach. The story explains what they do to clean it up.

Ask questions such as:

- Where were the family in the story going?
- Why were they upset?
- How did they clean up the mess?
- Why is it important to keep the beach clean?
- Have you ever cleaned up a messy place? Tell about what you did.

Take-Home Books

Use these simple directions to make reproducible take-home books for each of the five sections of *The Ocean*.

1. Reproduce the book pages for each child.
2. Cut the pages along the cut lines.
3. Place the pages in order, or this may be done as a sequencing activity with children. Guide children in assembling the book page by page.
4. Staple the book together.

After making each take-home book, review the story as children turn the pages of their own books. Send the storybook home along with the Parent Letter on page 5.

Dear Parent(s) or Guardian(s),

As part of our unit *The Ocean*, I will be presenting five storybooks to the class. Your child will receive a take-home storybook for you to share. Remember that reading to children helps them develop a love of reading. Regularly reading aloud to children has proven to enhance a variety of early language skills including:

- vocabulary and concept development,
- letter recognition,
- phonemic awareness,
- auditory and visual discrimination, and
- left to right tracking.

I hope you enjoy sharing these stories with your child.

As you read to your child, remember to:

1. speak clearly and with interest.
2. track words by moving your finger under each word as you read it.
3. ask your child to help you identify objects in the pictures. Talk about these objects together.
4. discuss your own experiences as they relate to the story.
5. allow your child to express his or her own thoughts and ideas and to ask you questions.

I hope you enjoy all five of these stories.

Sincerely,

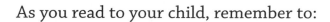

Storyboards

A storyboard is an excellent way to enhance vocabulary and concept development.

Each section of *The Ocean* includes full-color storyboard pieces to use in extending the language and concepts introduced. Ideas for using the storyboard pieces in each section are found on pages 7–9.

Turn the full-color cutouts into pieces that will adhere to a flannel- or felt-covered storyboard. Just laminate the pieces and affix self-sticking Velcro® dots to the back of each piece.

The Ocean
pages 29–33

Near the Shore
pages 67 and 69

In the Deep Ocean
pages 103 and 105

How We Move on the Ocean
pages 145–149

Taking Care of the Ocean
pages 179 and 181

Section One
The Ocean

"Maggie's Trip to the Ocean" Storyboard Use the colorful storyboard pieces on pages 29–33 to follow up your presentation of the story "Maggie's Trip to the Ocean." You may choose to use the following teacher script to present the story:

Today we are going to talk about some of the animals Maggie saw on her trip to the ocean. Place each animal and plant around the edge of the board one at a time and review its name.

- *This is seaweed. It grows in a tide pool.*
- *This is a sea star. It grows in a tide pool.*

Repeat until all of the items that can be found in a tide pool have been selected.

Remove the tide pool, placing the plants and animals back around the edge of the board.

Repeat with the kelp forest. Remind children that some of the same animals that are in the tide pool can be found in the kelp forest.

Remove the storyboard pieces and allow children to replace each piece as they retell the story.

Section Two
Near the Shore

"1, 2, 3 What Do You See?" Storyboard Use the colorful storyboard pieces on pages 67 and 69 to follow up your presentation of the story "1, 2, 3 What Do You See?" You may choose to use the following teacher script to present the story:

Here is the kelp forest under the sea. Let's name the animals that live in the kelp forest. Place each set of animals one at a time on the storyboard. Name each animal as it is placed.

- *This is an octopus.*
- *These are otters,* etc.

Lay the number cards along one edge. Invite children to count each different kind of animal and place the correct number by the animals on the storyboard. *Let's count the otters. One, two. That's right. There are two otters. Who can find two for me?* Put the numeral 2 by the otters. Continue until all of the animals have been counted and all numbers are in place.

Remove the storyboard pieces and allow children to replace each piece as they retell the story.

Storyboards

Section Three
In the Deep Ocean

"I Live in the Ocean" Storyboard After reading "I Live in the Ocean," discuss the animals from the story using the storyboard pieces on pages 103 and 105. You may choose to use the following teacher script to present the story:

> *Let's talk about animals that live out in the ocean.* Place the whale on the storyboard.

> • *This is a whale. A whale flips its tail up and down when it swims.*

> *Can you use your hand to show me how the whale's tail moves? That's right. It moves up and down. A whale breathes air like we do. It has to come to the surface of the water to get its air.* Continue with each animal from the story. Involve students by asking them to imitate some action of each animal as it is discussed.

Remove the storyboard pieces and allow children to replace each piece as they retell the story.

Section Four
How We Move on the Ocean

"Sailing, Sailing" Storyboard Use the storyboard pieces on pages 145–149 to follow up your presentation of the story "Sailing, Sailing." You may choose to use the following teacher script to present the story:

> *The people in this story are having fun on the water. They are riding in different kinds of vehicles. The animals in this story are watching the people. Let's use these pictures to match the animal and the vehicle it saw.*

> Place the surfboard on the storyboard. *This is a surfboard.* Place the hermit crab next to the surfboard. *The hermit crab saw the surfboard.* Continue until all of the vehicles and animals are on the storyboard.

> *Let's tell the story using the pictures.* Point to each vehicle and animal. Encourage children to join in as you say, *The hermit crab saw the surfboard. The gull saw the sailboat,* etc.

Remove the storyboard pieces and allow children to replace each piece as they retell the story.

Section Five
Taking Care of the Ocean

"Clean It Up" Storyboard Use the storyboard pieces on pages 179 and 181 to follow up your presentation of the story "Clean It Up!" Children will match the characters from the story with the items they collected as they cleaned up the beach.

Place all of the characters across the top of the storyboard. Place the items found at the beach along the bottom of the board. Take one character at a time and place it in the middle of the board. *This is Dad. What did he clean up at the beach? That's right. He cleaned up the plastic rings.* Call on a child to put the plastic rings next to Dad. Continue with Mom, Tasha, Jamal, and Kim.

Place the garbage can and the recycle can on the storyboard. *This is a recycling can. We put things in here that can be used again. What should we put in the recycling can? That's right. The cans (bottles, plastic rings) go in the recycling can. This is a garbage can. What should we put in the garbage can? Yes. The papers should go in the garbage can.*

Point to the remaining items at the bottom of the board. *Should we throw the shells in the garbage or recycling can? No. They belong at the beach.* Repeat with the seaweed and pebbles. *We should leave things that are a part of the ocean at the beach.*

Remove the storyboard pieces and allow children to replace each piece as they retell the story.

Creating an Atmosphere

Create a delightful ocean environment in your classroom. Feature the positional words you are developing in the unit. You may also use this area to display children's work. Use a large plastic tub with some sand and shells to display books about the sea.

Make an Ocean Bulletin Board

• Staple yellow butcher paper on the board as a backing.
• Cut waves along the top of blue butcher paper. Staple the blue paper over the yellow backing.

All About the Ocean • EMC 2407 • ©2005 by Evan-Moor Corp.

Simple Steps to Show You How

Ship

- Cut out a ship from blue, white, red, and black construction paper. Add details with a marker.

- Tape the pieces together and slip the ship behind the blue waves of the backing paper.

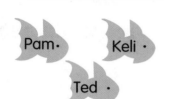

School of Fish

- Cut out a colorful fish for each child in your class. Write their names on the fish.

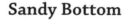

Sandy Bottom

- Cut a strip from a large brown paper bag. Crinkle it up to add texture. Pin it to the bulletin board.

Sea Stars

- Cut sea stars from purple construction paper and pin them along the sand.

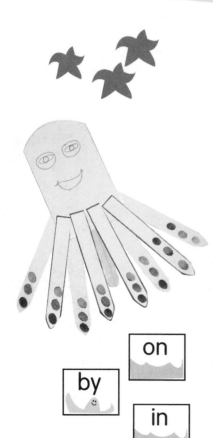

Octopus

- Display the children's Ocean Puppets art projects (page 107).

Bulletin Board Title

- Label the board with large cutout letters—**The Ocean**.

Positional Word Cards

- Print the positional words *on, in,* and *by* on white cards. Draw picture clues to identify the words for nonreaders.

The Ocean

Children are presented with an introduction to the ocean
and an overview of plants and animals that live in the ocean.

Maggie's Trip to the Ocean

Maggie went to the ocean.
Maggie went to the sea.
Maggie went to the ocean
to see what she could see.

Maggie peeked in the ocean.
Maggie peeked in the sea.
Maggie peeked in the ocean
to see what she could see.

2

Maggie swam in the ocean.
Maggie swam in the sea.

Maggie swam in the ocean
to see what she could see.

Maggie dived in ocean.
Maggie dived in the sea.
Maggie dived in the ocean
to see what she could see.

6

7

Come with me to the ocean.
Come with me to the sea.
Come with me to the ocean.
Let's see what we can see.

8

The End

Note: Teachers will make copies and cut in half for minibooks.

Maggie's Trip to the Ocean

Maggie went
to the ocean.
Maggie went
to the sea.
Maggie went
to the ocean
to see what
she could see.

1

Maggie peeked
in the ocean.
Maggie peeked
in the sea.
Maggie peeked
in the ocean
to see what
she could see.

2

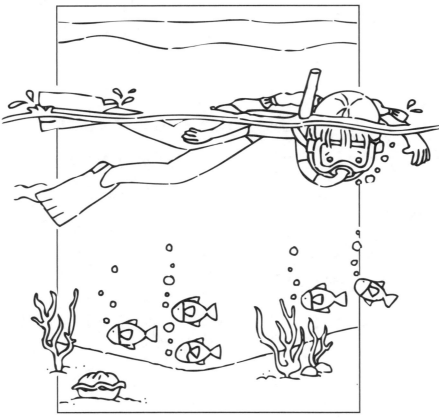

Maggie swam
in the ocean.
Maggie swam
in the sea.
Maggie swam
in the ocean
to see what
she could see.

3

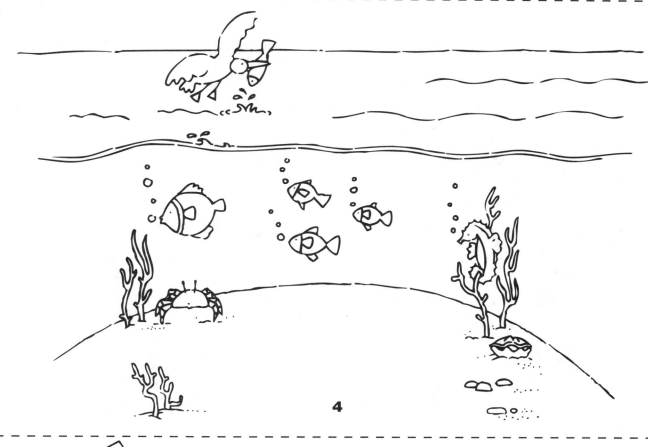

4

Maggie dived
in the ocean.
Maggie dived
in the sea.
Maggie dived
in the ocean
to see what
she could see.

5

6

7

Come with me
to the ocean.
Come with me
to the sea.
Come with me
to the ocean.
Let's see what
we can see.

8

The End

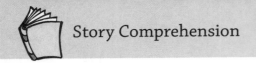

Note: Children color plants and animals that are found in the ocean.

Name _____

Did Maggie See It?

Color the plants and animals
that live in the ocean.

Note: See page 7 for suggestions on using the storyboard pieces on pages 29–33 for Maggie's Trip to the Ocean.

Storyboard Pieces

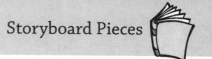

The Ocean

©2005 by Evan-Moor Corp.
All About the Ocean
EMC 2407

The Ocean

©2005 by Evan-Moor Corp.
All About the Ocean
EMC 2407

The Ocean

©2005 by Evan-Moor Corp.
All About the Ocean
EMC 2407

The Ocean

©2005 by Evan-Moor Corp.
All About the Ocean
EMC 2407

The Ocean

©2005 by Evan-Moor Corp.
All About the Ocean
EMC 2407

The Ocean

©2005 by Evan-Moor Corp.
All About the Ocean
EMC 2407

The Ocean

©2005 by Evan-Moor Corp.
All About the Ocean
EMC 2407

The Ocean

©2005 by Evan-Moor Corp.
All About the Ocean
EMC 2407

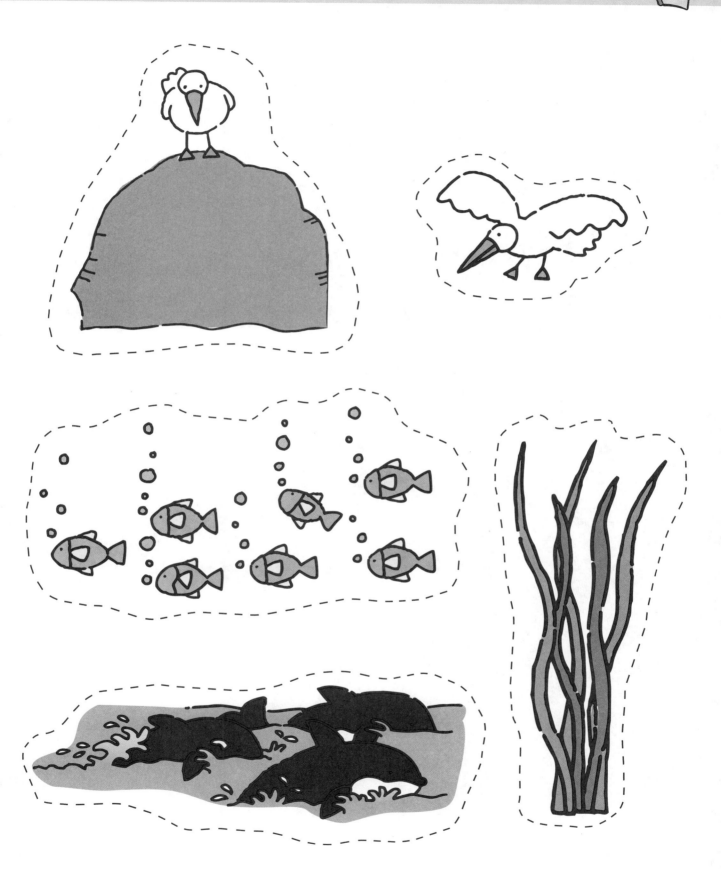

The Ocean

The Ocean

The Ocean

The Ocean

The Ocean

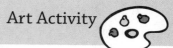

Children create a colorful underwater scene of the ocean.

Materials

- white art paper, one sheet per child
- colored construction paper, one sheet per child
- crayons
- blue tempera paint, thinned with water
- paintbrushes
- glue

Crayon-Resist Ocean

Steps to Follow

1. Children draw and color their own underwater scenes on a sheet of white art paper. Encourage children to color each area heavily so that their drawing will hold up better when the wash is brushed over it.

2. Children paint over the picture with the blue wash. Allow the paintings to dry.

3. Assist children in framing their paintings.

4. Display the finished paintings for everyone to enjoy.

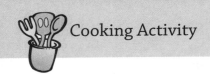
Note: Check for allergies before beginning any cooking activity. An allergic reaction can occur through taste, smell, or contact with allergens.

Salty or Not?

Preparation

1. Place each type of food to sample on a separate plate.

2. Prepare a paper plate for each child to sort his or her food onto. Reproduce the icons below. Cut them apart and tape the "salty" icon on the left side of the paper plate and the "not salty" icon on the right side.

3. Fill two glasses with water. Add salt to one glass of water and stir until it is dissolved.

Steps to Follow

1. Explain to children that water in the ocean is salty. Show children the two glasses of water. Allow children to taste the water to see which one is salty like the ocean. (Each child will use two plastic spoons to taste only the water that clings to the spoon.) Mix the glasses up for each child.

2. Distribute the paper plates. Explain that children will place salty foods on the side of the plate with the *salty* icon, and non-salty foods on the side with the *not salty* icon.

3. Children go to the food table, take one sample of each food, take a little bite, and decide where it goes on their plates.

4. Once everyone has taken a turn tasting and sorting the foods, compare results. Call on volunteers to tell which foods were salty and which foods were not.

Children will take a bite of several items, placing each one in the correct category: "salty" or "not salty."

Materials

- two glasses of fresh water
- salt
- plastic spoons, two per child
- paper plates, one per child
- black marking pen
- saltine crackers
- salt-free crackers
- salted pretzels
- carrot sticks
- potato chips
- fruit wedges
- Optional: salted and unsalted nuts*
  *allergy alert

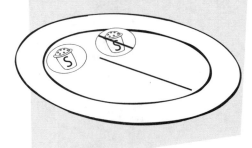

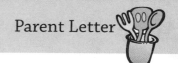

Dear Parent(s) or Guardian(s),

Today we learned that ocean water is salty. We tasted water and foods and decided which were salty and which were not. Besides having fun eating, the children practiced these skills:

- listening to and following directions
- vocabulary and concept development
- categorizing
- using small motor skills

For our unit *The Ocean,* we will send home a variety of new recipes. Each recipe will be one that your child has tried in class and is excited about. We hope you have an opportunity to try this recipe again with your child. Allowing your child to help in the kitchen is a wonderful way to reinforce learning skills while creating family memories.

Salty or Not?

Materials

- two plates
- saltine crackers
- salt-free crackers
- salted pretzels
- carrot sticks
- potato chips
- fruit wedges
- Optional: salted and unsalted nuts

Steps to Follow

1. Give your child two plates, one for salty foods and one for foods that are not salty.

2. Provide samples of the foods listed at left (or other salty and non-salty foods from your cupboard).

3. Have your child taste each food and decide if it tastes salty or not. Have him or her place all salty things on one plate and non-salty things on the other.

4. Ask your child, "Is the ocean's water salty or not salty?"

In, On, or By?

Steps to Follow

1. Make cards that say *in, on,* and *by*. Explain to children that you will be talking about the words on the cards.

2. Point to the word *in* and have children look around the room to find things that are in other things (ball in ball box, etc.).

3. Point to the word *on* and have children look around the room to find things that are on other things (book on table, etc.).

4. Point to the word *by* and have children look around the room to find things that are by other things (Matthew is by the door, etc.).

5. Distribute the activity sheet on page 39 and guide children through it as they mark the location of the octopus in each picture.

Materials

- page 39, reproduced, one per child

- The Ocean bulletin board (see pages 10 and 11)

- index cards

 All About the Ocean • EMC 2407 • ©2005 by Evan-Moor Corp.

Note: Children circle the positional word that describes where the octopus is.

Language—Vocabulary Development

Name _____

In, On, or By?

Circle the word that tells where you see the octopus.

in   on   by

in   on   by

in   on   by

in   on   by

Name _____

It Starts Like Fish

Color the pictures that begin like **fish**.

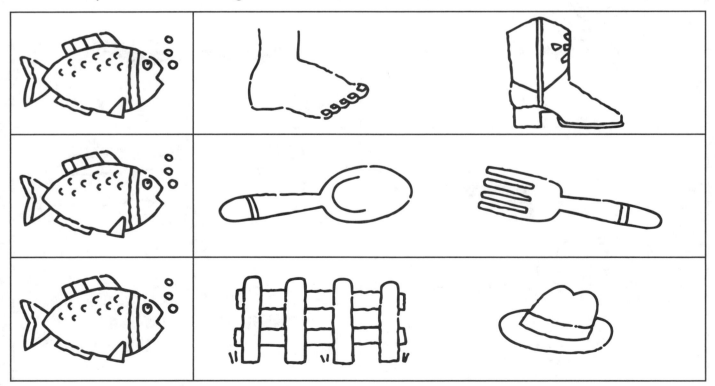

Note: Children count the fish and trace the numbers in the fish. Then they write the total number of fish.

Math—Counting 123

Name _____

A School of Fish

Count the fish. Trace.

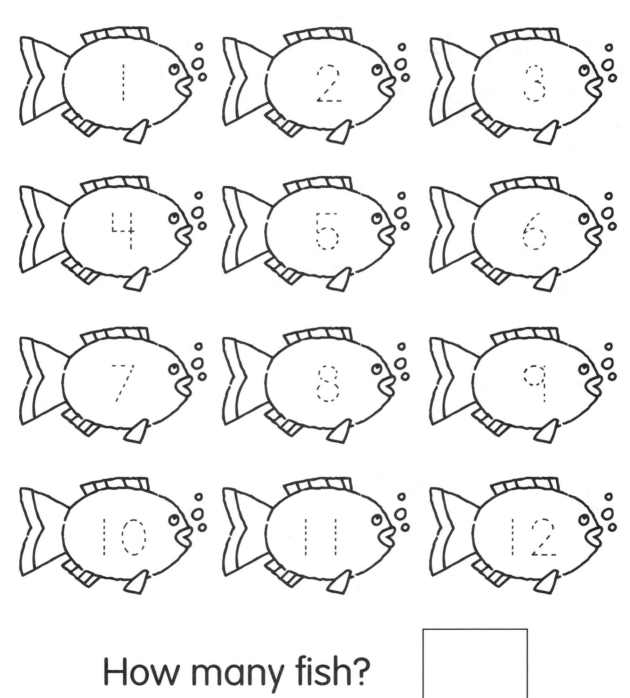

How many fish?

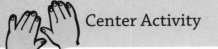

Working in pairs, children sort the shells into different groups.

Sorting Seashells

Creating the Center

1. Laminate and cut apart pages 43 and 45 or use real seashells. If you use real shells, provide variations that can be sorted by size (large, medium, small), shape (round, triangular, oval, etc.), and color (three different colors).

2. Prepare the center by covering the bottom of a large cookie sheet with rough sandpaper (or real sand) to represent the beach. Place the seashells on the tray.

3. Plan time to model how the center is used.

Using the Center

1. Show children the tray of shells. Discuss ways in which the shells are different. Model one way the shells can be sorted.

2. Children work in pairs at the center. Each child takes a turn sorting the shells and then explaining to a partner how he or she sorted the shells. Children continue sorting the shells in different ways.

Materials

• pages 43 and 45, laminated

• large cookie sheet

• sand or sandpaper

• Optional: real seashells

Sorting Seashells

©2005 by Evan-Moor Corp.
All About the Ocean • EMC 2407

Sorting Seashells

©2005 by Evan-Moor Corp.
All About the Ocean • EMC 2407

Sorting Seashells

©2005 by Evan-Moor Corp.
All About the Ocean • EMC 2407

Sorting Seashells

©2005 by Evan-Moor Corp.
All About the Ocean • EMC 2407

Sorting Seashells

©2005 by Evan-Moor Corp.
All About the Ocean • EMC 2407

Sorting Seashells

©2005 by Evan-Moor Corp.
All About the Ocean • EMC 2407

Sorting Seashells

©2005 by Evan-Moor Corp.
All About the Ocean • EMC 2407

Sorting Seashells

©2005 by Evan-Moor Corp.
All About the Ocean • EMC 2407

Sorting Seashells

©2005 by Evan-Moor Corp.
All About the Ocean • EMC 2407

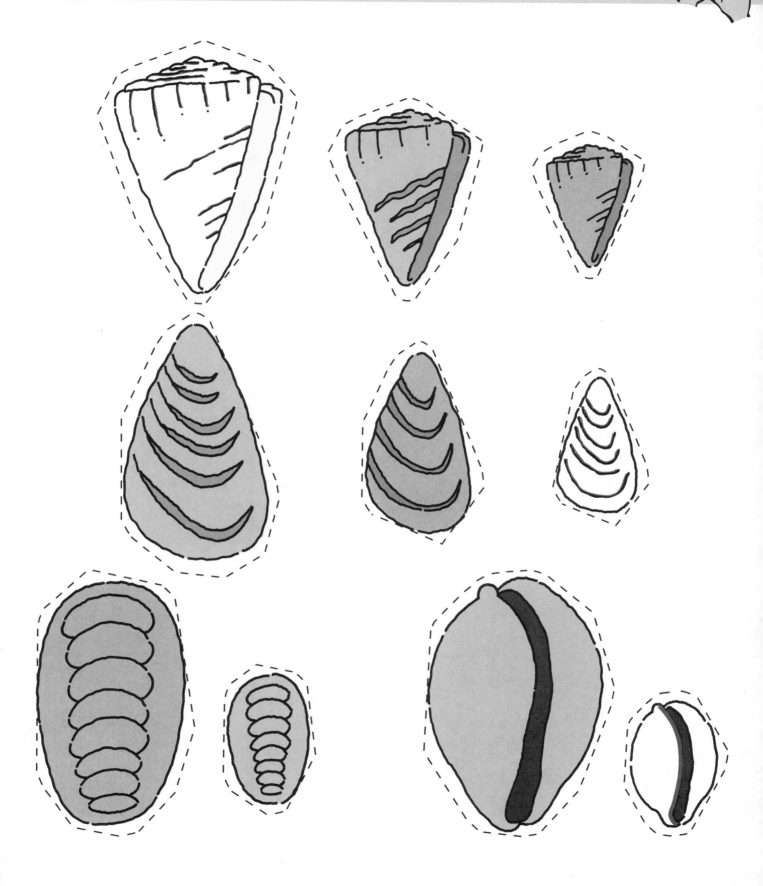

Sorting Seashells

©2005 by Evan-Moor Corp.
All About the Ocean
EMC 2407

Sorting Seashells

©2005 by
Evan-Moor Corp.
All About the Ocean
EMC 2407

Sorting Seashells

©2005 by
Evan-Moor Corp.
All About the Ocean
EMC 2407

Sorting Seashells

©2005 by
Evan-Moor Corp.
All About the Ocean
EMC 2407

Sorting Seashells

©2005 by
Evan-Moor Corp.
All About the Ocean
EMC 2407

Sorting Seashells

©2005 by
Evan-Moor Corp.
All About the Ocean
EMC 2407

Sorting Seashells

©2005 by Evan-Moor Corp.
All About the Ocean
EMC 2407

Sorting Seashells

©2005 by
Evan-Moor Corp.
All About the Ocean
EMC 2407

Sorting Seashells

©2005 by
Evan-Moor Corp.
All About the Ocean
EMC 2407

Sorting Seashells

©2005 by Evan-Moor Corp.
All About the Ocean
EMC 2407

Children imitate the movement of various sea creatures as they play this variation of Follow the Leader.

Follow the Sea Creature

How to Play

1. Children form a line on the playground, standing about an arm's length apart from each other.

2. Select a leader. The leader says, *I am a (crab). Follow me.* Then he or she starts off across the playground, imitating the action of the named sea creature.

3. The other children follow along, imitating the same action.

4. Select a different leader. The leader chooses a different animal to imitate, and the other children then follow along.

5. Repeat until all the children have been the leader.

I am a crab. Follow me.

"A Sailor Went to Sea" Clapping Rhyme

Children sing this repetitive rhyme while performing a fun clapping pattern.

A sailor went to
    sea, sea, sea
To see what he could
    see, see, see.

But all that he could
    see, see, see
Was the bottom of the deep blue
    sea, sea, sea.

Clapping Pattern:

A—Clap your own hands.

sai—Clap right hands with a partner.

lor—Clap your own hands.

went—Clap left hands with a partner.

to—Clap your own hands.

sea—Clap both your partner's hands three times.

Repeat motions for the rest of the rhyme.

All About the Ocean • EMC 2407 • ©2005 by Evan-Moor Corp.

Note: Sing this song to the tune of "The Wheels on the Bus."
Invite children to think of a third verse for this song.

Music/Dramatic Play Activity

Children invent movements to accompany this seafaring tune.

The Waves at Sea

The waves at sea go up and down,
Up and down,
Up and down.
The waves at sea go up and down,
Up—and—down.

The fish at sea go swim, swim, swim,
Swim, swim, swim,
Swim, swim, swim.
The fish at sea go swim, swim, swim,
Swim—swim—swim.

Near the Shore

Children learn about the plants and animals
living in the tide pools and the kelp forests of the ocean.

1, 2, 3 What Do You See?

1 octopus
hiding in the water
near the seashore

2 otters playing in the water near the seashore

2

3 anemones
sitting in the water
near the seashore

4 sea stars
resting in the water
near the seashore

5 barnacles
waving in the water
near the seashore

6 hermit crabs
crawling in the water
near the seashore

6

7 little fish
swimming in the water
near the seashore

What a busy place!

The End

Note: Teachers will make copies and cut in half for minibooks.

1, 2, 3
What Do
You See?

1 octopus

hiding in the water

near the seashore

1

2 otters

playing in the water

near the seashore

2

3 anemones

sitting in the water

near the seashore

3

4 sea stars
resting in the water
near the seashore

4

5 barnacles
waving in the water
near the seashore

5

6 hermit crabs crawling in the water near the seashore

6

7 little fish swimming in the water near the seashore

7

What a busy place!

8

The End

Name _____

Near the Seashore

Count. Glue.

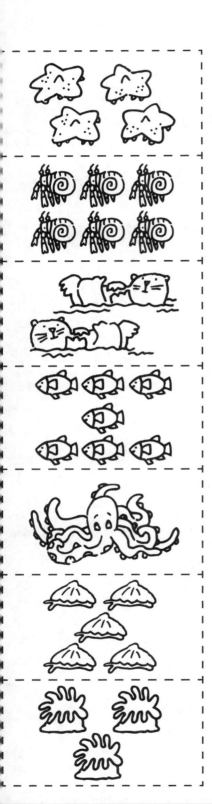

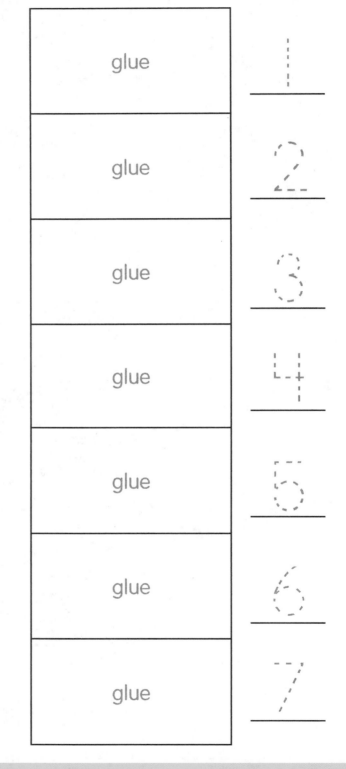

Note: See page 7 for suggestions on using the storyboard pieces on pages 67 and 69 for 1, 2, 3 What Do You See?

Storyboard Pieces

Near the Shore

Near the Shore

Near the Shore

Near the Shore

Near the Shore

Near the Shore

Near the Shore

Near the Shore

Near the Shore

Near the Shore

Near the Shore

Near the Shore

Near the Shore

Near the Shore

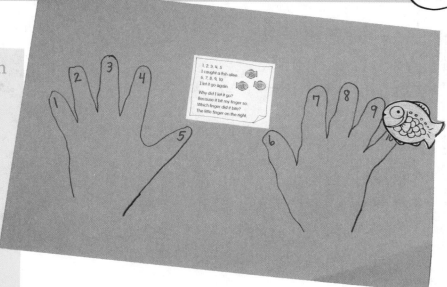

Children "catch a fish" on their little finger while they recite a counting rhyme.

Materials

- page 72, reproduced, one rhyme and one fish per child
- colored construction paper, one sheet per child
- crayons
- glue
- scissors

I Caught a Fish

Preparation

1. Teach children the rhyme on page 72.
2. Prepare an art center with all materials assembled.
3. Reproduce page 72 several times. Each child needs one rhyme and one fish.
4. Model a completed I Caught a Fish project.

Steps to Follow

1. Working in pairs, children trace around each other's hands on a sheet of colored construction paper.
2. Then they number their fingertips from 1 to 10.
3. Children color then glue one little fish (page 72) to "the little finger on the right."
4. They glue the rhyme onto the construction paper above their hands.
5. Children recite the rhyme and use their picture as a prop.

Note: Reproduce this rhyme and pattern to use with I Caught a Fish art activity. Children raise one finger at a time as they recite the rhyme.

1, 2, 3, 4, 5
I caught a fish alive.
6, 7, 8, 9, 10
I let it go again.

Why did I let it go?
Because it bit my finger so.
Which finger did it bite?
The little finger on the right.

1, 2, 3, 4, 5
I caught a fish alive.
6, 7, 8, 9, 10
I let it go again.

Why did I let it go?
Because it bit my finger so.
Which finger did it bite?
The little finger on the right.

1, 2, 3, 4, 5
I caught a fish alive.
6, 7, 8, 9, 10
I let it go again.

Why did I let it go?
Because it bit my finger so.
Which finger did it bite?
The little finger on the right.

Note: Check for allergies before beginning any cooking activity.
An allergic reaction can occur through taste, smell, or contact with allergens.

Cooking Activity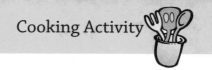

Seven Little Fish in the Blue Ocean

Children create their own blue ocean with seven little fish.

Materials

- Berry Blue Jell-O® (or other blue gelatin)
- water
- mixing bowl
- measuring cup
- ladle
- gummy fish, seven per child
- small clear plastic cups, one per child
- cookie sheets
- black marking pen
- plastic spoons, one per child
- access to a microwave oven or hot plate
- access to a refrigerator

Preparation

1. Prepare a cooking center with all materials assembled.
2. Mix the gelatin ingredients just prior to beginning this cooking activity. Do <u>not</u> refrigerate.

Steps to Follow

1. Children write their names on a plastic cup (assist children as needed).
2. Then they take turns ladling the blue gelatin into their cups (assist children as needed).
3. Children set their cup on a cookie sheet.
4. An adult places the gelatin in the refrigerator until it is partially set. This will take about an hour.
5. Once the gelatin is partially set, children count out seven gummy fish to drop into their cups.
6. An adult returns the cups to the refrigerator to fully set.
7. Enjoy eating the "seven little fish in the blue ocean."

Variation

If you don't have access to a refrigerator, it can be just as much fun for children to count out seven goldfish crackers (especially if you use the multicolored variety) onto a small blue paper plate "ocean."

Dear Parent(s) or Guardian(s),

Today we cooked in class. Your child prepared "Seven Little Fish in the Blue Ocean." Besides having fun cooking and eating, the children practiced these skills:

- vocabulary development
- following directions
- using small motor skills

For our unit *The Ocean,* we will send home a variety of new recipes. Each recipe will be one that your child has tried in class and is excited about. We hope you have an opportunity to try this recipe again with your child. Allowing your child to help in the kitchen is a wonderful way to reinforce learning skills while creating family memories.

Seven Little Fish in the Blue Ocean

Materials

- Berry Blue Jell-O® (or other blue gelatin)
- water
- measuring cup
- mixing bowl
- ladle
- gummy fish (7 per cup)
- small clear plastic cups

Steps to Follow

1. Mix the gelatin per instructions. You may have your child add the cool water to help with this step. Have your child ladle the gelatin into clear cups. Set the gelatin in the refrigerator until it is partially set (about one hour).

2. When the gelatin is partially set, have your child count out seven gummy fish to drop into each cup.

3. Return the cups to the refrigerator to fully set.

4. Enjoy eating the "seven little fish in the blue ocean."

Note: Explain to children that sea horses are a type of fish that hide in sea grass. Children move the sea horse to the sea grass by coloring boxes with the word *fish*.

Language—Word Recognition

Name _____

To the Sea Grass

Help the sea horse get to the sea grass.
Color the boxes with the word **fish**.

fish	sand	water	crab	sand
fish	crab	sand	sand	water
fish	fish	water	crab	sand
sand	fish	fish	fish	water
water	crab	sand	fish	fish
crab	sand	water	sand	fish

Note: Children complete each pattern by cutting and gluing the pictures below.

Name _____

In a Row

Cut. ✂ Glue.

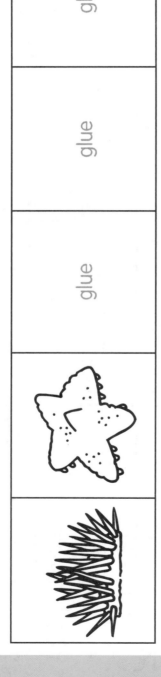

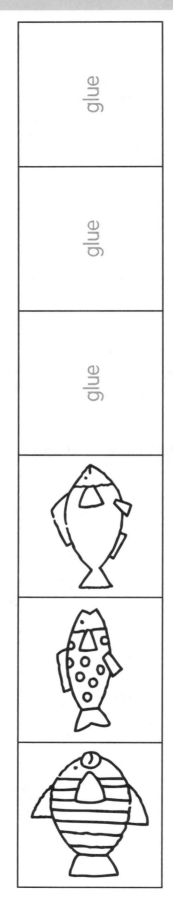

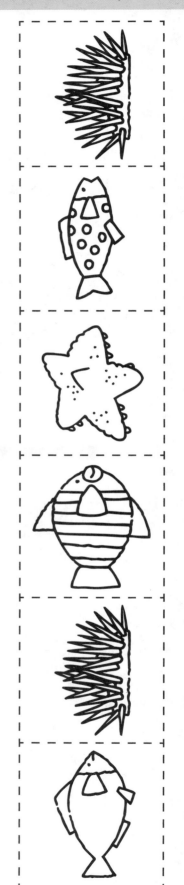

All About the Ocean • EMC 2407 • ©2005 by Evan-Moor Corp.

Note: Guide children through the steps for making a graph using the information in the fish tank.

Math—Counting; Graphing

Name _____

How Many Do You See?

Count. Color a box for each fish and snail.

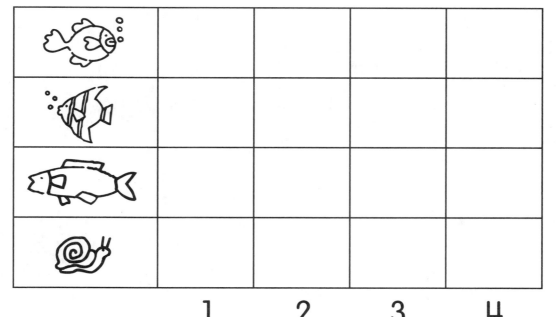

1   2   3   4

Which has the most?

Working independently or in pairs, children match the two ocean animals or plants that are the same.

In the Ocean Match

Creating the Center

1. Laminate and cut out the cards on pages 79 and 81.
2. Place the cards in a sturdy folder or envelope.
3. Plan time to model how the center is used.

Using the Center

1. Children match the ocean animal and plant cards correctly.
2. Once all the cards have been matched, children mix up the cards, turn the cards facedown, and then choose two cards to turn over. If the cards match, the child puts them aside. If the cards do not match, the child turns them facedown and continues to try to make matches (like the game Concentration).

Materials

- pages 79 and 81, laminated
- scissors
- sturdy folder or envelope

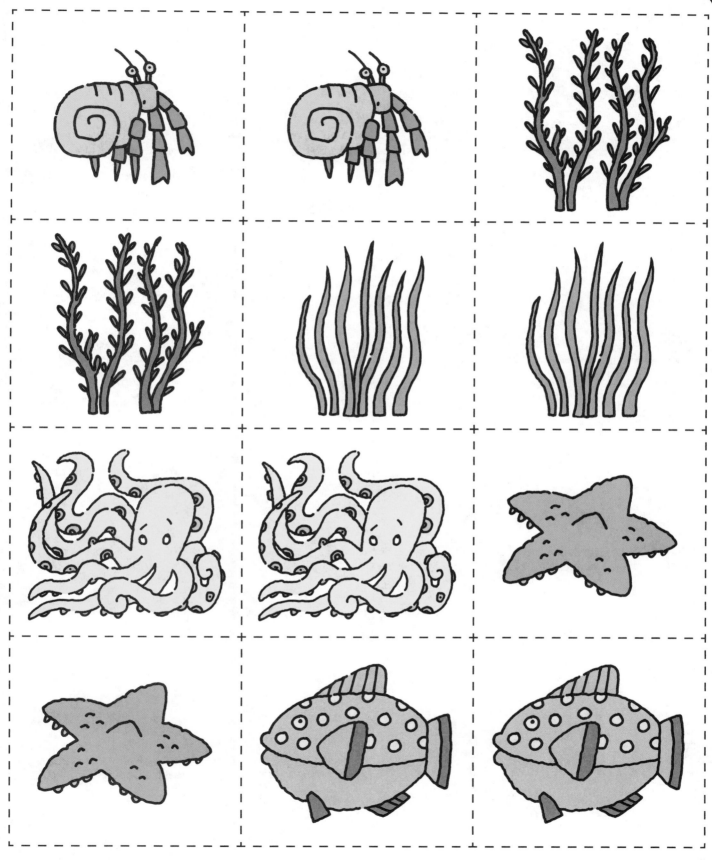

In the Ocean Match

In the Ocean Match

In the Ocean Match

In the Ocean Match

In the Ocean Match

In the Ocean Match

In the Ocean Match

In the Ocean Match

In the Ocean Match

In the Ocean Match

In the Ocean Match

In the Ocean Match

In the Ocean Match

In the Ocean Match

In the Ocean Match

In the Ocean Match

In the Ocean Match

In the Ocean Match

In the Ocean Match

In the Ocean Match

In the Ocean Match

In the Ocean Match

In the Ocean Match

In the Ocean Match

Catch the Jellyfish

Children head outdoors for a game of catch using colorful "jellyfish" balls.

Materials

- soft balls such as Nerf® balls, one for each pair of children

- permanent black marking pen

Preparation

1. Using a permanent black marker, draw a jellyfish on each of the balls.

2. Show the balls to the children. Explain that jellyfish are soft like the balls. Tell children that they will be trying to "catch the jellyfish."

3. Plan to play in a large outdoor space.

How to Play

1. Take the class outside. Divide the class into pairs (if you have an extra child, have one group of three).

2. Children play catch, taking turns throwing and catching their "jellyfish."

Extension

Have children take a step backwards every time they successfully complete a catch.

In the Ocean

Preparation

Once children have learned the verses, have them incorporate movement to the song.

Steps to Follow

1. Children practice singing "In the Ocean."

2. They sing the song and act out the way each creature moves.

3. Children think of other sea creatures to include in the song. When a child names a creature, classmates act out the way it moves.

Children sing this fun song as they imitate the way each creature moves.

Materials

• page 85

Note: Sing this song to the tune of "The Wheels on the Bus."

Music/Dramatic Play Activity

In the Ocean

The fish in the ocean go swish, swish, swish,
 swish, swish, swish,
 swish, swish, swish.
The fish in the ocean go swish, swish, swish,
Down in the water.

Verse 2

The crabs in the ocean go crawl, crawl,…

Verse 3

The eels in the ocean go wiggle, wiggle, wiggle,…

Verse 4

The clams in the ocean go squirt, squirt, squirt,…

Verse 5

The limpets in the ocean go wave, wave, wave,…

Verse 6

The otters in the water go swim, swim, swim,…

In the Deep Ocean

Children learn about animals
found in the open ocean.

I Live in the Ocean

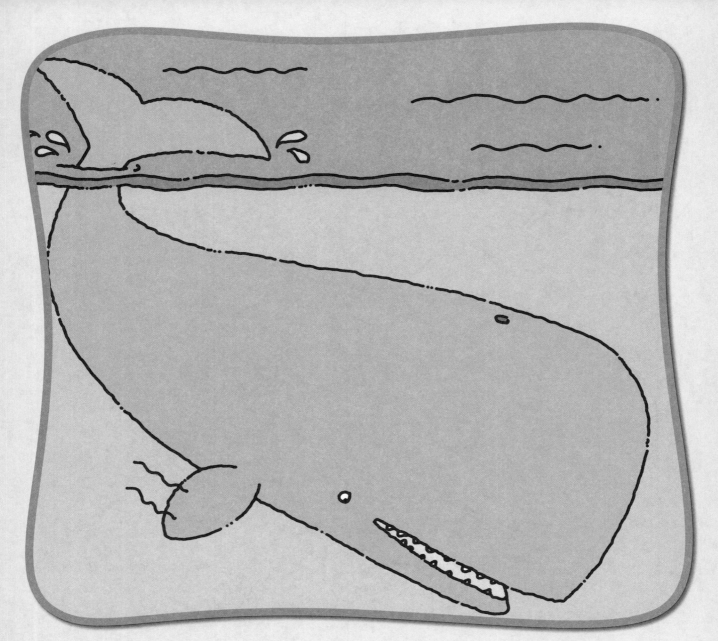

Hi.

I'm a whale.

I live in the ocean.

I flip my tail up and down to swim.

I come up for air.

I dive down for food.

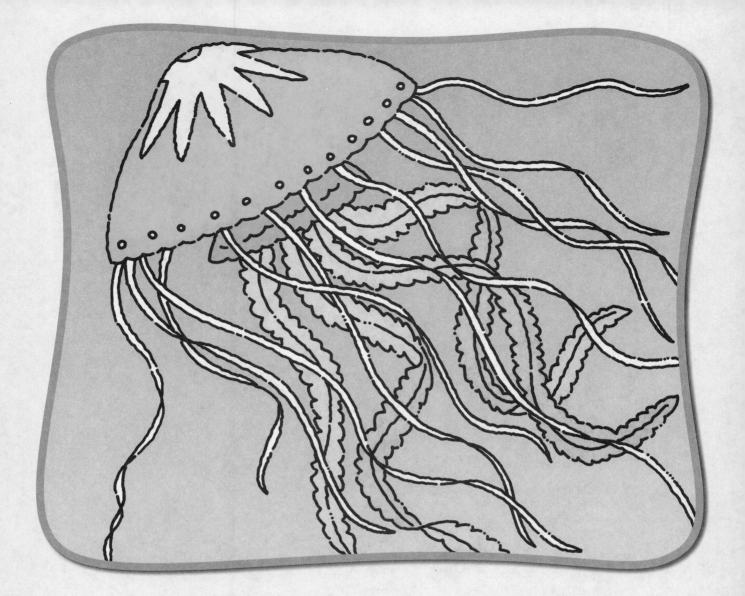

Hi.

I'm a jellyfish.

I live in the ocean.

I float along in the water.

I have a soft body.

I have long tentacles.

I catch fish with my tentacles.

Hi.

I'm a shark.

I live in the ocean.

I move my tail from side to side to swim.

I use my eyes and nose to find food.

I use my sharp teeth to catch food.

Hi.

I'm a giant octopus.

I live in the ocean.

I can crawl and swim.

I have a soft body.

My skin can change color.

I catch food with my tentacles.

Hi.

I'm a ray.

I live in the ocean.

I swim along in the water.

I open my mouth when I swim.

I catch food in my mouth.

Hi.

I'm a sea turtle.

I live in the ocean.

I use my flippers to paddle in the water.

I have a thick shell.

It protects my soft body.

I use my sharp beak to catch my food.

6

Hi.

We are fish.

We live in the ocean.

We move our fins to swim.

We swim together to keep safe.

Hi.

We are krill.

We live in the ocean.

We are very, very small.

We are food for some big animals.
Whales and some big fish eat us.

8

The End

Note: Teachers will make copies and cut in half for minibooks.

Reproducible Story

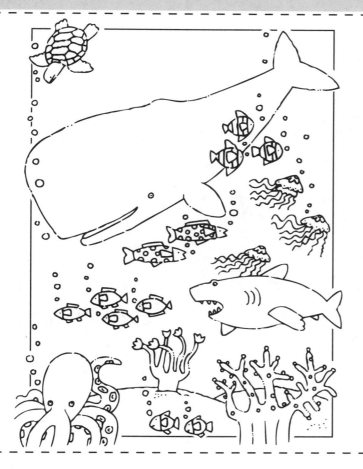

I Live in the
Ocean

Hi.

I'm a whale.

I live in the ocean.

I flip my tail up and down to swim.

I come up for air.

I dive down for food.

1

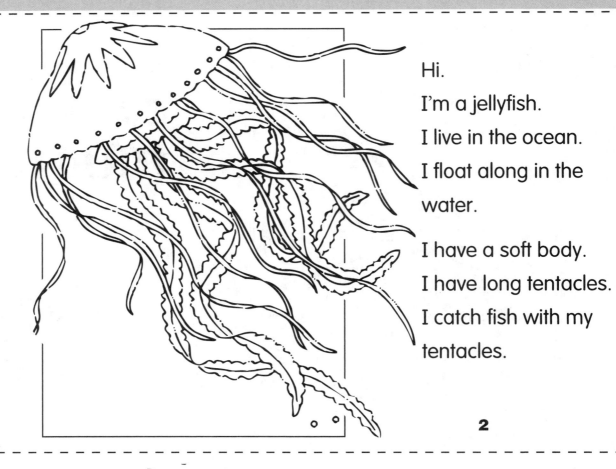

Hi.

I'm a jellyfish.

I live in the ocean.

I float along in the water.

I have a soft body.

I have long tentacles.

I catch fish with my tentacles.

2

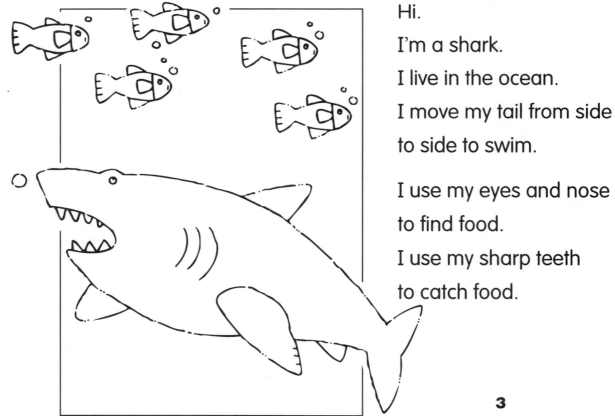

Hi.

I'm a shark.

I live in the ocean.

I move my tail from side to side to swim.

I use my eyes and nose to find food.

I use my sharp teeth to catch food.

3

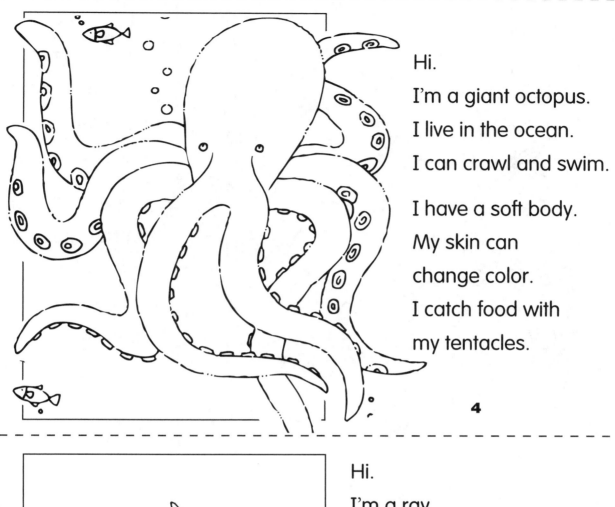

Hi.

I'm a giant octopus.

I live in the ocean.

I can crawl and swim.

I have a soft body.
My skin can
change color.
I catch food with
my tentacles.

4

Hi.

I'm a ray.

I live in the ocean.

I swim along in the water.

I open my mouth
when I swim.
I catch food
in my mouth.

5

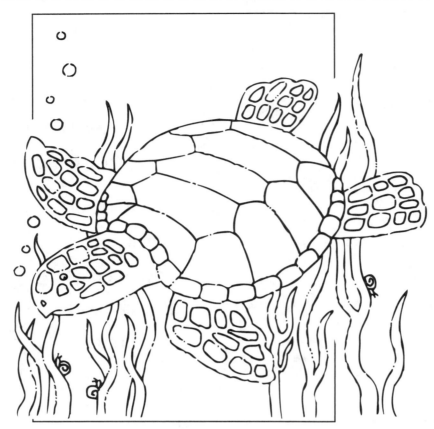

Hi.

I'm a sea turtle.

I live in the ocean.

I use my flippers to

paddle in the water.

I have a thick shell.

It protects my

soft body.

I use my sharp

beak to catch

my food.

6

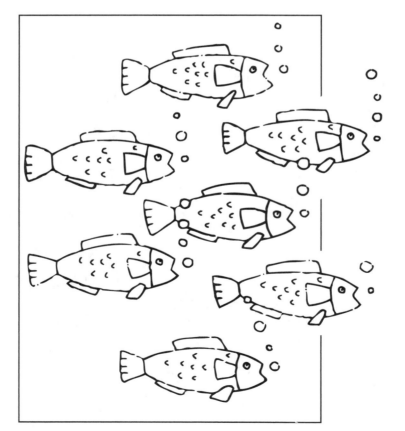

Hi.

We are fish.

We live in the ocean.

We move our

fins to swim.

We swim together

to keep safe.

7

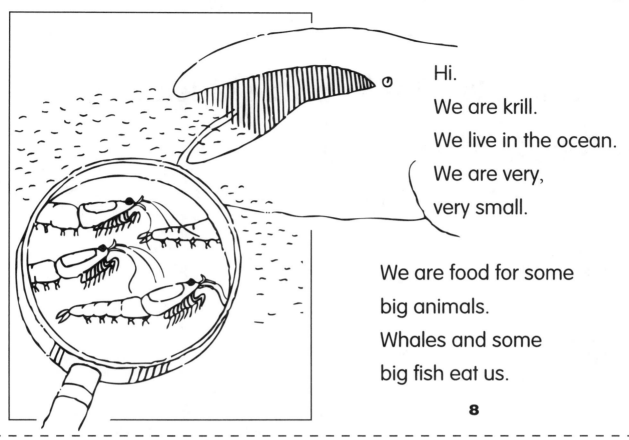

Hi.
We are krill.
We live in the ocean.
We are very,
very small.

We are food for some
big animals.
Whales and some
big fish eat us.

8

The End

Note: Children cut out pictures of animals that live in the ocean and glue them to the ocean scene below.

Name _____

We Live in the Ocean

Color. Cut. Glue.

All About the Ocean • EMC 2407 • ©2005 by Evan-Moor Corp.

Note: See page 8 for suggestions on using the storyboard pieces on pages 103 and 105 for I Live in the Ocean.

Storyboard Pieces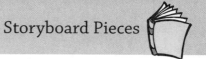

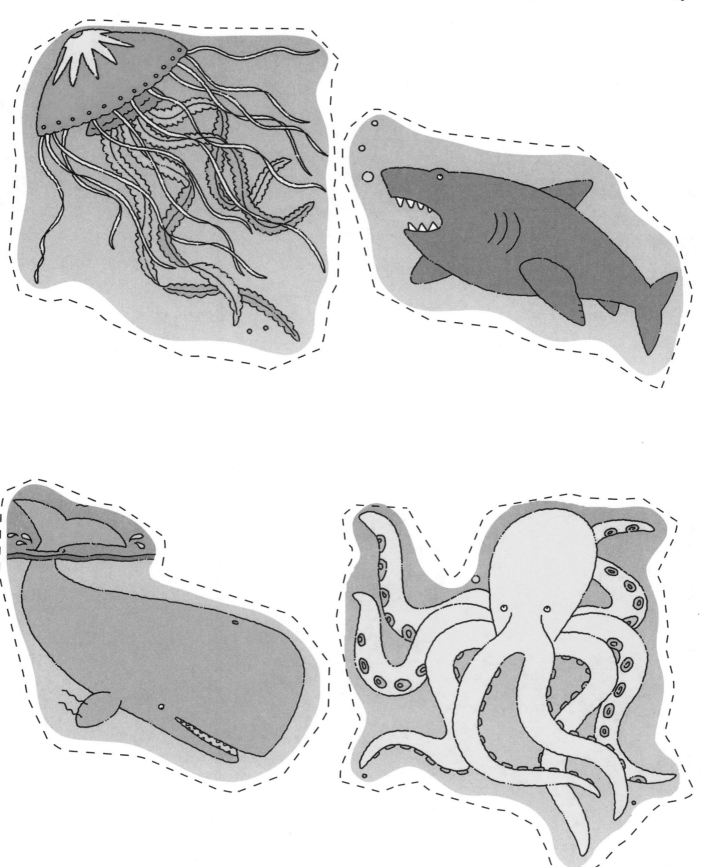

In the Deep Ocean

©2005 by Evan-Moor Corp.
All About the Ocean
EMC 2407

In the Deep Ocean

©2005 by Evan-Moor Corp.
All About the Ocean
EMC 2407

In the Deep Ocean

©2005 by Evan-Moor Corp.
All About the Ocean
EMC 2407

In the Deep Ocean

©2005 by Evan-Moor Corp.
All About the Ocean
EMC 2407

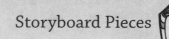

In the Deep Ocean

In the Deep Ocean

In the Deep Ocean

In the Deep Ocean

Ocean Puppets

After making either of these delightful puppets, encourage children to put on a class-wide puppet show.

Whale Materials

- pages 108 and 109, reproduced on blue construction paper
- crayons or marking pens
- scissors
- craft sticks, one per child
- glue

Octopus Materials

- pages 108 and 110, reproduced on pink construction paper
- crayons or marking pens
- scissors
- craft sticks, one per child
- glue
- ink pad

Preparation

1. Reproduce pages 108 and 109 on blue construction paper, one per puppet.
2. Reproduce pages 108 and 110 on pink construction paper, one per puppet.
3. Model a completed Whale Puppet and a completed Octopus Puppet.

Steps to Follow

Whale

1. Children cut out the body pattern and fold it in half. Then they cut out the whale tail and glue it into the end of the body pattern.
2. Next, they glue the body pattern edges together.
3. Then children cut out the spout, color it a darker blue, and glue it to the top of the whale.
4. Then they add a mouth and eyes with crayons or marking pens.
5. Finally, children glue a craft stick to the bottom of the puppet.

Octopus

1. Children cut out the body pattern and fold it in half. Then they put glue along all edges of the pattern, insert a craft stick, and press it closed.
2. Next, children cut out the tentacles and glue them around the bottom of the octopus body. Using their fingertips and an ink pad, they make "suckers" on each tentacle.
3. Then children add a mouth and eyes with crayons or marking pens.

Note: Reproduce this pattern to use with Ocean Puppets art activity.

Body Pattern

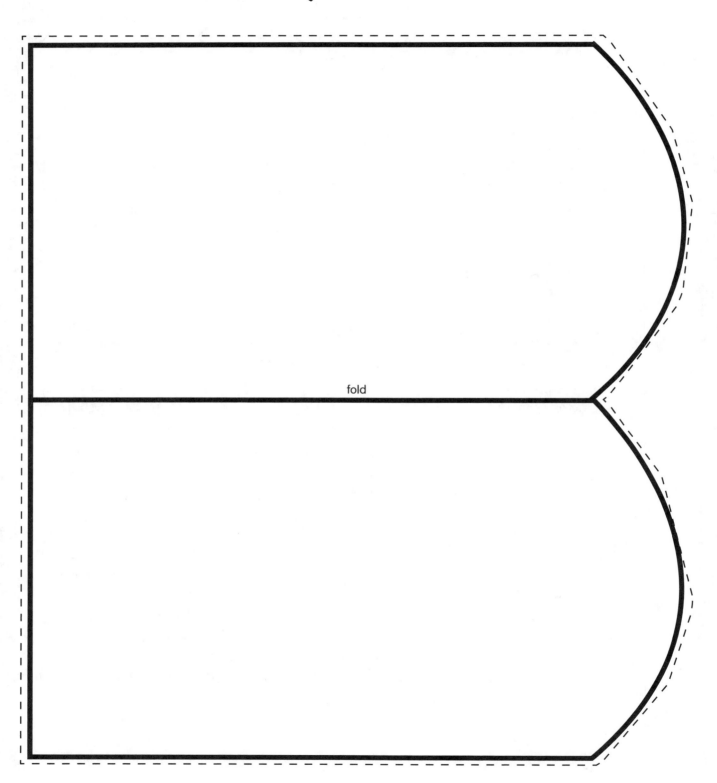

fold

Note: Reproduce these patterns to use with Ocean Puppets art activity.

Art Activity Pattern Pieces

Whale Tail and Water Spout

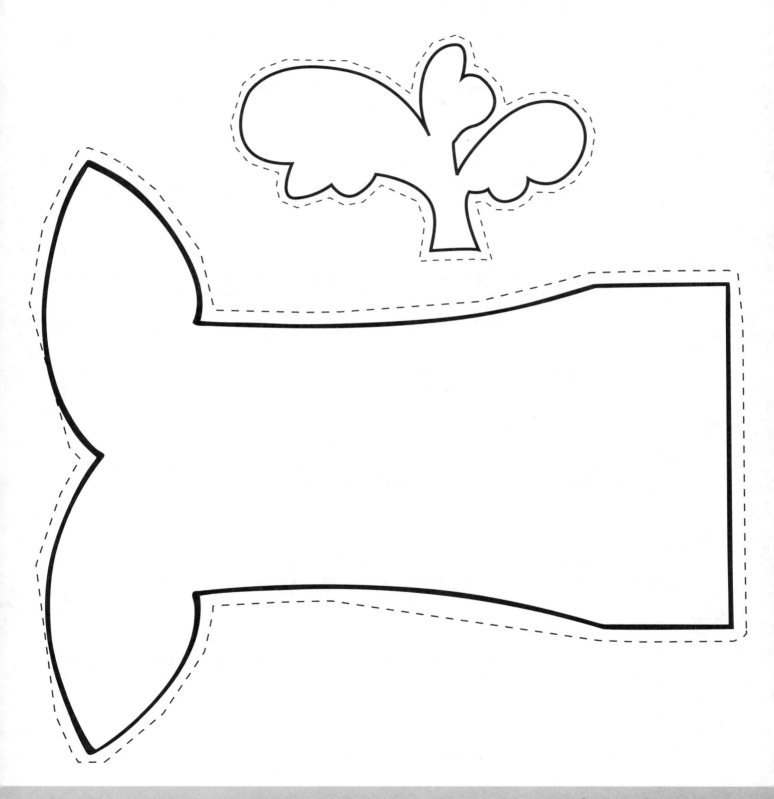

Note: Reproduce these patterns to use with Ocean Puppets art activity.

Octopus Tentacles

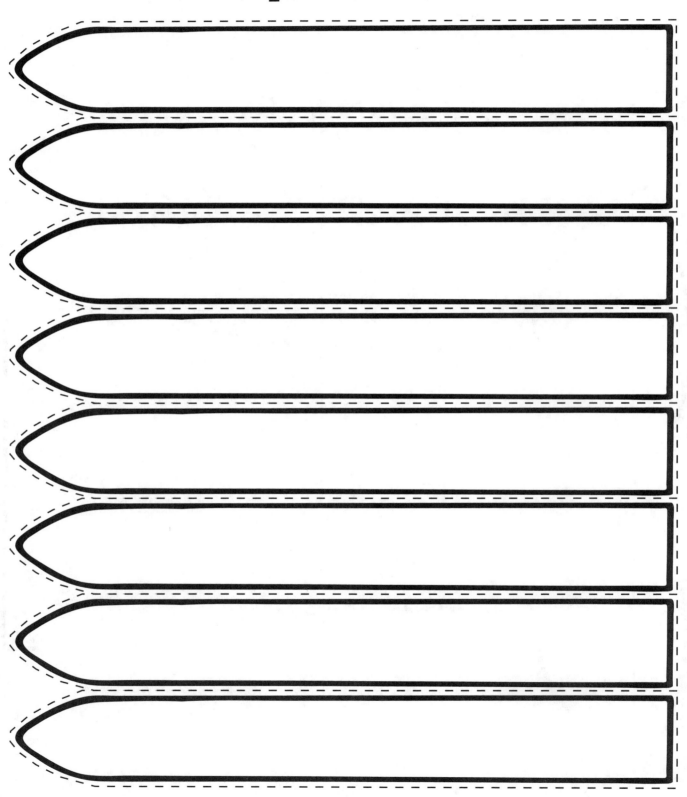

Note: Check for allergies before beginning any cooking activity. An allergic reaction can occur through taste, smell, or contact with allergens.

Cooking Activity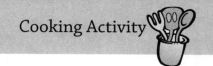

Children taste a favorite from the ocean, "Tuna Triangles."

Tuna Triangles

Materials

- page 112, laminated
- canned tuna
- mayonnaise
- bread (cut into triangles)
- relish
- chopped celery
- plastic or paper bowls (for ingredients)
- spoons (tablespoons and teaspoons)
- plate
- small plastic cups
- plastic spoons and dull plastic knives
- small paper plates
- napkins

Preparation

1. Set out bowls containing the various ingredients and a plate containing bread triangles.
2. Laminate the Tuna Triangles Recipe Chart on page 112. Place it in the cooking center for children's reference.

Steps to Follow

1. Allow a few children at a time to come up and prepare their tuna triangles.
2. While children are preparing their sandwiches, discuss things we eat that come from the sea. Show pictures of a tuna, shrimp, etc., as you conduct the discussion.
3. Once everyone has made a Tuna Triangle, enjoy your tasty snack!

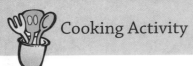

Tuna Triangles

①

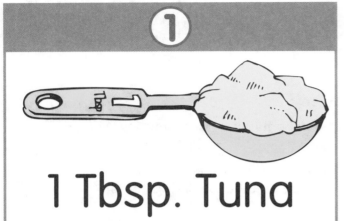

1 Tbsp. Tuna

②

1 tsp. mayo

③

1 tsp. pickle

④

1 tsp. celery

⑤

stir it up

⑥

spread it

Dear Parent(s) or Guardian(s),

Today we cooked in class. Your child helped prepare "Tuna Triangles." Besides having fun cooking and eating, the children practiced these skills:

• listening to and following directions

• vocabulary and concept development

• measurement

• using small motor skills

For our unit *The Ocean*, we will send home a variety of new recipes. Each recipe will be one that your child has tried in class and is excited about. We hope you have an opportunity to try this recipe again with your child. Allowing your child to help in the kitchen is a wonderful way to reinforce learning skills while creating family memories.

Tuna Triangles

Materials

• canned tuna

• mayonnaise

• bread (cut into triangles)

• relish

• chopped celery

• bowls (for ingredients)

• spoons (tablespoons and teaspoons)

• small mixing bowl

• spoon and dull plastic knife

• small plates

• napkins

Steps to Follow

1. Have your child place the ingredients below in a bowl. (Quantities will depend on how much you are making.)

   • tuna

   • mayonnaise

   • relish

   • celery

2. Have your child stir the ingredients together.

3. Cut slices of bread into triangles.

4. Have your child help spread tuna on the bread triangles.

5. Enjoy your snack!

Name _____

Sea Rhymes

Draw a line to match the pictures that rhyme.

Note: Review color words with children. Lead the class in using crayons to fill in the color key below. Then children follow the key to color the picture.

Language—Word Recognition

Colorful Fish

Complete the color key.
Color the picture.

◯ red   ◯ yellow   ◯ blue

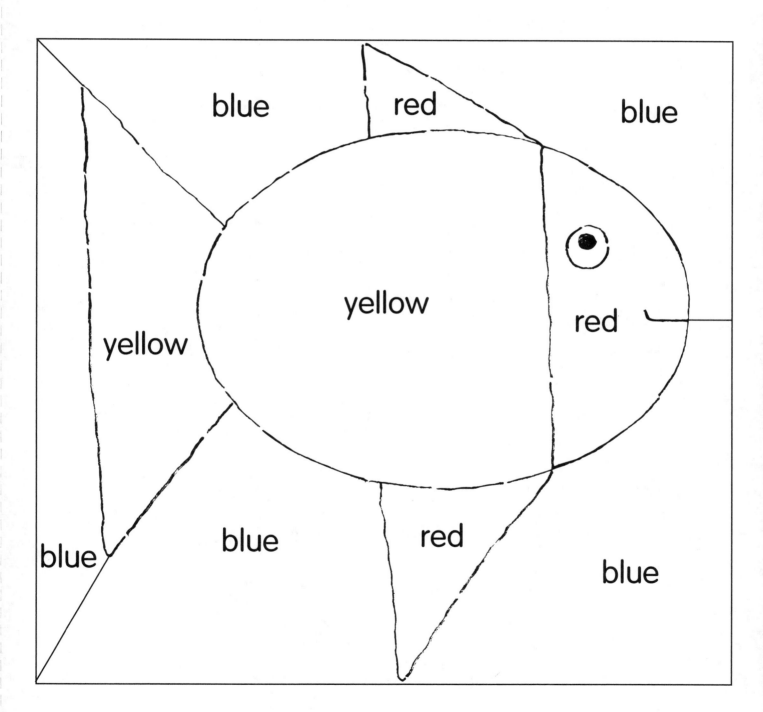

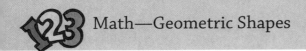
Note: Lead the class in using crayons to fill in the color key below. Review the names of the geometric shapes. Children follow the key to color the pictures.

Name _____

Find the Shapes

Color the shapes.

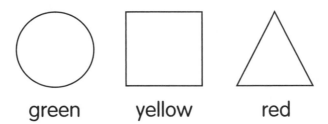

green   yellow   red

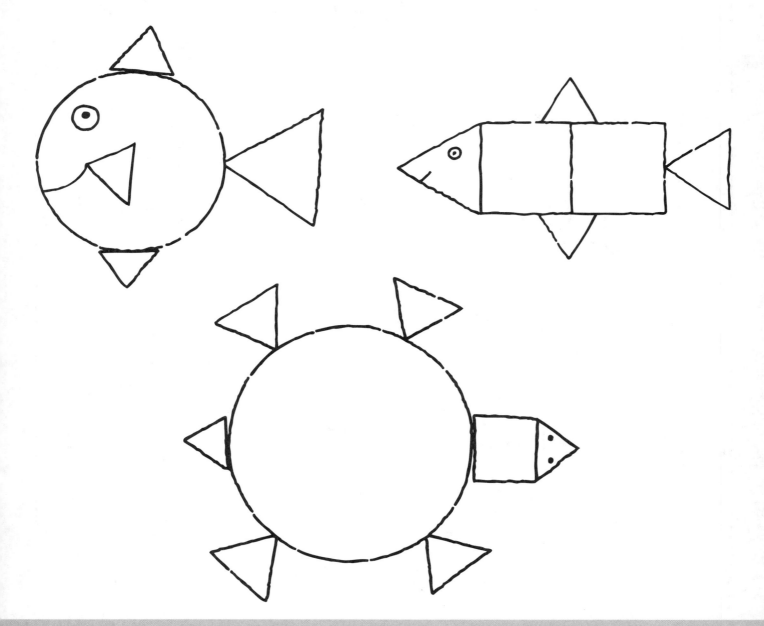

Name _____

Count the Jellyfish

Number the jellyfish.

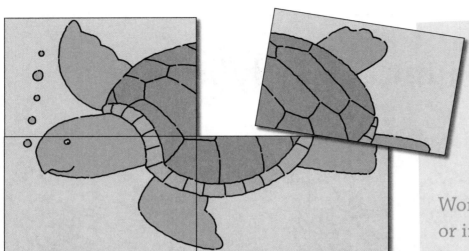

Ocean Puzzles

Working independently or in pairs, children put together ocean puzzles.

Creating the Center

1. Laminate and cut apart the puzzle pieces on pages 119 and 121.

2. Place each puzzle in its own envelope. Label the envelopes.

3. Place the puzzle envelopes in a sturdy folder or envelope.

4. Plan time to model how the center is used.

Using the Center

Using the center individually or with a partner, children put together one or more of the puzzles.

Materials

• pages 119 and 121, laminated

• scissors

• four envelopes to store the puzzles

• sturdy folder or envelope

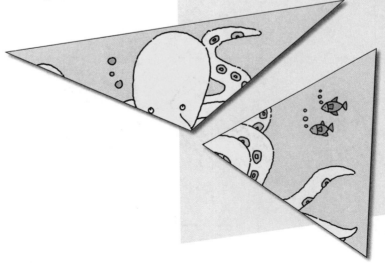

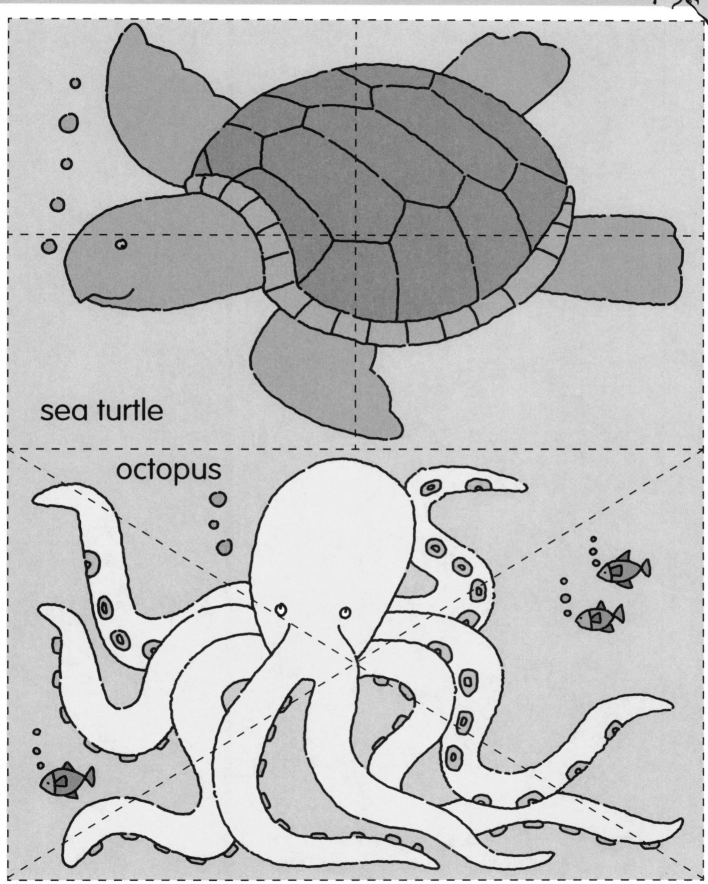

sea turtle

octopus

Ocean Puzzles

©2005 by Evan-Moor Corp.
All About the Ocean
EMC 2407

Ocean Puzzles

©2005 by Evan-Moor Corp.
All About the Ocean
EMC 2407

Ocean Puzzles

©2005 by Evan-Moor Corp.
All About the Ocean
EMC 2407

Ocean Puzzles

©2005 by Evan-Moor Corp.
All About the Ocean
EMC 2407

Ocean Puzzles

©2005 by Evan-Moor Corp.
All About the Ocean
EMC 2407

Ocean Puzzles

©2005 by Evan-Moor Corp.
All About the Ocean
EMC 2407

Ocean Puzzles

©2005 by Evan-Moor Corp.
All About the Ocean
EMC 2407

Ocean Puzzles

©2005 by Evan-Moor Corp.
All About the Ocean
EMC 2407

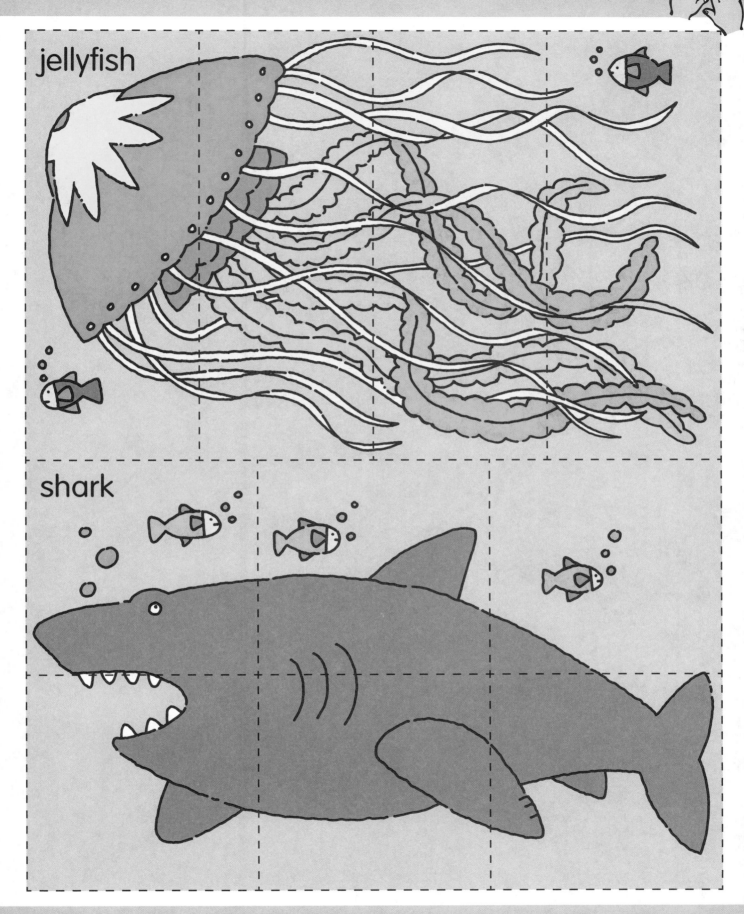

jellyfish

shark

Ocean Puzzles

Ocean Puzzles

Ocean Puzzles

Ocean Puzzles

Ocean Puzzles

Ocean Puzzles

Ocean Puzzles

Ocean Puzzles

Ocean Puzzles

Ocean Puzzles

Swim, Fish, Swim is played like Duck, Duck, Goose.

Swim, Fish, Swim

How to Play

1. Children sit cross-legged in a circle.

2. Select a child to be "It."

3. The child who is It walks around the outside of the circle, gently tapping each person on the head and calling him or her "Fish."

4. As soon as It taps a child and calls him or her "Shark," that child must get up and chase It around the circle. It has to try to get into the Shark's spot before being tagged.

5. If the Shark tags It before he or she is safely in the Shark's spot, It must sit in the middle of the circle, and the Shark becomes It for the next round.

6. The player in the center must remain there until another player is tagged.

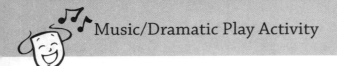

Note: Sing this song to the tune of "For He's a Jolly Good Fellow."

The Shark Swam over the Ocean

The shark swam over the ocean,

The shark swam over the ocean,

The shark swam over the ocean,

　　To see what it could see.

The other side of the ocean,

The other side of the ocean,

The other side of the ocean,

　　Was all that it could see.

　　Was all that it could see,

　　Was all that it could see,

The other side of the ocean,

Was all that it could see!

Verse 2

The whale dived into the ocean,…

　　To see what it could see.

The bottom of the ocean,…

　　Was all that it could see!

Children imitate the motions for **swim** and **dive** as they sing the verses.

All About the Ocean • EMC 2407 • ©2005 by Evan-Moor Corp.

Children practice counting as they sing or recite this rhyme.

Materials

- page 126, reproduced, one per child
- marking pens or crayons

One Hungry Jellyfish

How to Play

1. Each child colors a jellyfish picture. As children are coloring, the teacher walks around and tells them which number, 1 through 10, to write in the box on their jellyfish. Continue until each child has numbered their jellyfish.

2. Children sit in a row and sing "One Hungry Jellyfish." As they sing, each child stands as the number on their jellyfish is said.

3. You may wish to reproduce page 127 and use the leopard shark as a variant activity.

One hungry, two hungry,
Three hungry jellyfish,
Four hungry, five hungry,
Six hungry jellyfish,
Seven hungry, eight hungry,
Nine hungry jellyfish,
Ten of them can't sting me!

Verse 2

(Continue to count to 20 and sing above refrain.)

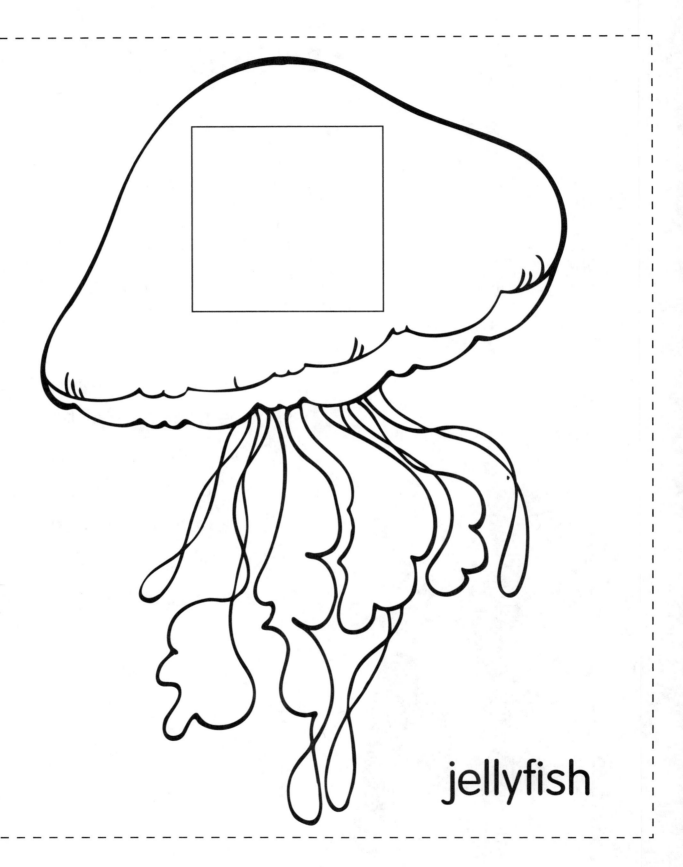

jellyfish

Note: Reproduce this picture for children to color, or use as an alternative to One Hungry Jellyfish. Instead, sing "One Hungry Shark."

Music/Dramatic Play Activity Pattern Piece

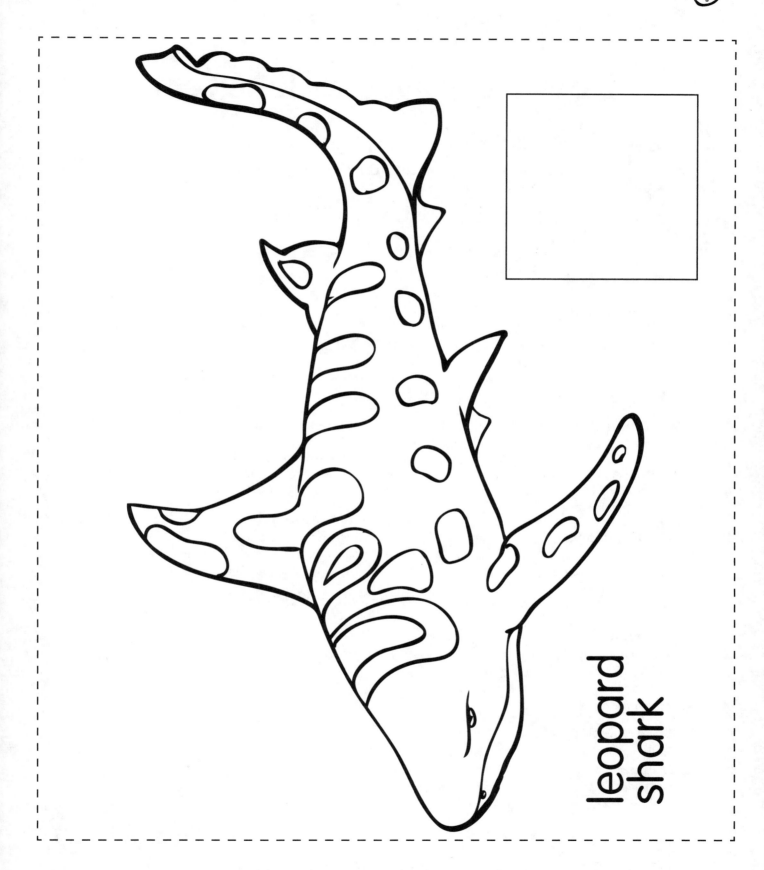

leopard shark

How We Move on the Ocean

Children learn about vehicles that
travel on the ocean and how they are used.

Sailing, Sailing

Hermit crab, hermit crab,
what do you see?
I see a surfboard riding on the sea.

1

Sea lion, sea lion, what do you see?
I see a tour boat sailing on the sea.

2

Little gull, little gull, what do you see?
I see a sailboat sailing on the sea.

3

Little seal, little seal, what do you see?
I see a kayak paddling on the sea.

4

Little fish, little fish, what do you see?
I see a fishing boat sailing on the sea.

5

Little whale, little whale, what do you see?
I see a big ship sailing on the sea.

6

Sea turtle, sea turtle, what do you see?
I see a submarine sailing under the sea.

7

Travelers, travelers, what do you see?
We see the animals in the sea.

8

The End

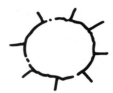

Sailing, Sailing

Hermit crab, hermit crab, what do you see? I see a surfboard riding on the sea.

1

Sea lion, sea lion,
what do you sea?
I see a tour boat
sailing on the sea.

2

Little gull, little gull,
what do you see?
I see a sailboat
sailing on the sea.

3

Little seal, little seal,
what do you see?
I see a kayak
paddling on the sea.

4

Little fish, little fish,
what do you see?
I see a fishing boat
sailing on the sea.

5

Little whale, little whale,
what do you see?
I see a big ship sailing
on the sea.

6

Sea turtle, sea turtle,
what do you see?
I see a submarine
sailing under the sea.

7

Travelers, travelers,
what do you see?
We see the
animals in the sea.

8

The End

How We Move on the Ocean **143**

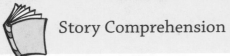

Story Comprehension

Note: Children color the pictures shown in Sailing, Sailing and make an *X* on what was not shown.

Name _____

Sailing, Sailing

Color the pictures from the story.

Make an **X** on what was <u>not</u> in the story.

All About the Ocean • EMC 2407 • ©2005 by Evan-Moor Corp.

Note: See page 8 for suggestions on using the storyboard pieces on pages 145–149 for How We Move on the Ocean.

Storyboard Pieces

How We Move
on the Ocean

How We Move
on the Ocean

How We Move
on the Ocean

How We Move
on the Ocean

How We Move
on the Ocean

How We Move
on the Ocean

©2005 by Evan-Moor Corp.
All About the Ocean
EMC 2407

How We Move
on the Ocean

©2005 by Evan-Moor Corp.
All About the Ocean
EMC 2407

How We Move on the Ocean **149**

**How We Move
on the Ocean**

©2005 by Evan-Moor Corp.
All About the Ocean
EMC 2407

**How We Move
on the Ocean**

©2005 by Evan-Moor Corp.
All About the Ocean
EMC 2407

**How We Move
on the Ocean**

©2005 by Evan-Moor Corp.
All About the Ocean
EMC 2407

**How We Move
on the Ocean**

©2005 by Evan-Moor Corp.
All About the Ocean
EMC 2407

**How We Move
on the Ocean**

©2005 by Evan-Moor Corp.
All About the Ocean
EMC 2407

**How We Move
on the Ocean**

©2005 by Evan-Moor Corp.
All About the Ocean
EMC 2407

**How We Move
on the Ocean**

©2005 by Evan-Moor Corp.
All About the Ocean
EMC 2407

Make a Sailboat

Steps to Follow

1. Children press a small ball of clay into the center of a plastic lid.

2. Then they tape the paper sail to a straw.

3. Next, children stick the straw into the clay and press the clay around the straw so it will stand up.

4. Allow two or three children at a time to place their sailboats in the water and blow against the sail to make them move.

Children create boats and sail them across a tub of water.

Materials

• sail pattern at right, reproduced, one per child

• plastic lids, one per child

• modeling clay, one small ball per child

• plastic straws, one per child

• tub of water

• tape

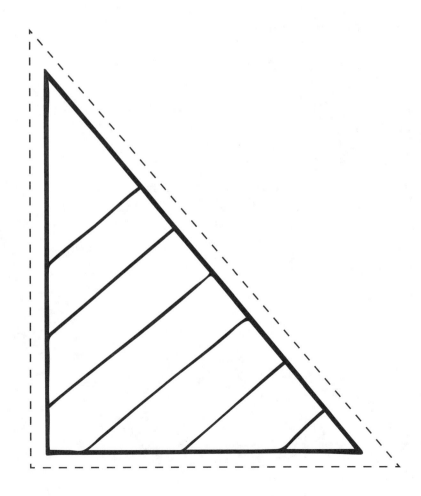

Sailboat Sandwiches

These simple but tasty sandwiches offer an opportunity to make a snack and practice geometric shapes at the same time.

Preparation

1. Trim the crusts off each piece of bread.

2. Plan time to model how to assemble a sailboat sandwich. Discuss the different shapes that a sailboat sandwich has. For example, the bread and the cheese are shaped like squares.

Steps to Follow

1. Children need one piece of bread, one piece of cheese, a plastic knife, and a paper plate.

2. Call children up a few at a time to make their sailboat sandwiches.

3. They spread butter on the piece of bread and slice the bread in half diagonally, as shown.

4. Children carefully slice the piece of cheese diagonally so that they have two triangles. They need only one triangle sail per sandwich. Allow them to munch on the extra sail as they work.

5. Children place the bottom edge of the cheese sail in between the bread pieces and place their sailboat on their blue paper plate ocean.

6. Once everyone has made a sandwich, review the geometric shapes before allowing the children to eat up!

Materials

- brown bread with crusts removed, one slice per child

- cheese slices, one slice per child

- butter

- blue paper plates

- dull plastic knives

- Optional: cook's aprons

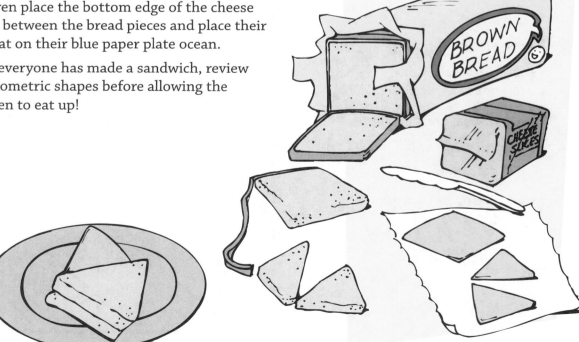

Dear Parent(s) or Guardian(s),

Today we cooked in class. Your child prepared a "Sailboat Sandwich." Besides having fun cooking and eating, the children practiced:

- vocabulary development
- listening to and following directions
- using small motor skills
- reviewing geometric shapes

For our unit *The Ocean,* we will send home a variety of new recipes. Each recipe will be one that your child has tried in class and is excited about. We hope you have an opportunity to try this recipe again with your child. Allowing your child to help in the kitchen is a wonderful way to reinforce learning skills while creating family memories.

Sailboat Sandwiches

Materials

- brown bread with crusts removed, one slice per person
- cheese slices, one slice per person
- butter
- blue paper plate
- dull plastic knife

Steps to Follow

1. Remove the crust from the bread in advance.
2. Let your child do the following:
   - cut the bread slice diagonally to make triangles
   - cut the cheese slice in half diagonally to make triangles (You need only one triangle sail for each sandwich.)
   - butter both pieces of bread
   - place the edge of the sail on one piece of bread
   - cover the edge of the sail with the other piece
   - place the sailboat on the blue paper plate ocean
3. Ask your child to name the shapes of the sailboat.
4. Enjoy the sandwich with a glass of milk or juice.

How Many Fish Can You Catch?

Children practice descriptive words and counting as they fish in pairs at this center.

Creating the Center

1. Laminate and cut apart the fish on page 155. Tape a paper clip at the mouth end of each fish.

2. Make the fishing poles by tying a string to one end of the pole and then tying a magnet to the string.

3. Place the fish in a blue tub or on blue butcher paper for the "ocean." Prepare a fishing area in your classroom.

4. Reproduce a supply of page 157 and keep them at the center.

5. Plan time to model how the center is used.

Using the Center

1. Two children take turns catching a fish by touching the magnet to the paper clip on the fish.

2. After catching a fish, each child describes the fish to his or her partner. *I caught a big blue fish.*

3. When all the fish have been caught, the children count how many they each have. *I caught four fish.*

4. Children complete page 157 after fishing at the center.

Materials

- page 155, laminated

- page 157, reproduced, one per child

- two pieces of doweling

- string

- paper clips

- tape

- two small magnets

- blue tub or blue butcher paper

   All About the Ocean • EMC 2407 • ©2005 by Evan-Moor Corp.

How Many Fish
Can You Catch?

©2005 by Evan-Moor Corp.
All About the Ocean
EMC 2407

How Many Fish
Can You Catch?

©2005 by Evan-Moor Corp.
All About the Ocean
EMC 2407

How Many Fish
Can You Catch?

©2005 by Evan-Moor Corp.
All About the Ocean
EMC 2407

How Many Fish
Can You Catch?

©2005 by Evan-Moor Corp.
All About the Ocean
EMC 2407

How Many Fish
Can You Catch?

©2005 by Evan-Moor Corp.
All About the Ocean
EMC 2407

How Many Fish
Can You Catch?

©2005 by Evan-Moor Corp.
All About the Ocean
EMC 2407

Name _____

How Many Fish Did You Catch?

Number the fish you caught.

Then cut and glue them into the ocean.

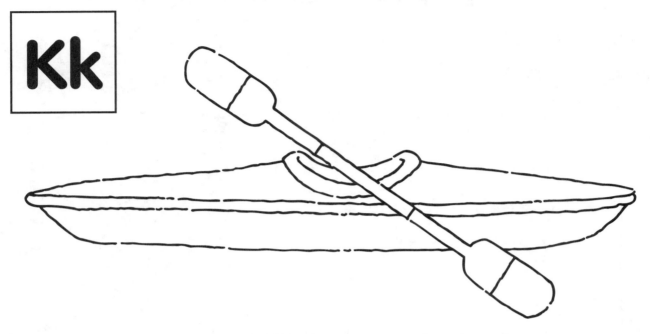ABC Language—Auditory Discrimination

Note: Name the pictures with children. They listen to the beginning sound and then color the pictures that begin with the same sound as *kayak*.

Name _____

Listen for the Sound

Kk

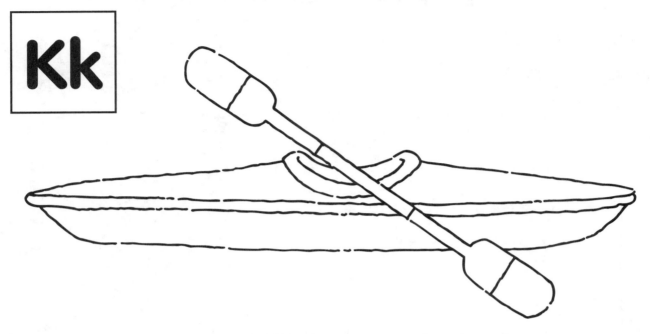

Color the pictures that begin with the same sound as **kayak**.

Note: Review ordinal numbers from first to fifth. Read each direction aloud, giving children enough time to color each boat before reading the next direction.

Math—Ordinal Numbers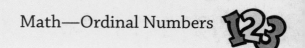

Name _____

Where Am I in Line?

Listen. Color.

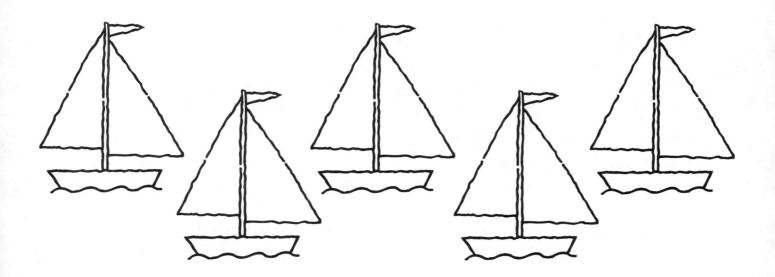

Color the 2nd boat green.

Color the 5th boat orange.

Color the 3rd boat blue.

Color the 1st boat purple.

Color the 4th boat red.

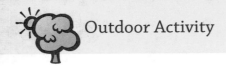

Stormy Weather

Stormy Weather is played like Upset the Fruit Basket.

Preparation

1. Reproduce the vehicle patterns at the bottom of this page to use as name tags for this outdoor game. Each child will wear a tag.

2. Color, laminate, and cut apart the tags. Punch a hole and add a yarn tie to each tag.

3. Use chalk to make a circle of large *X*'s on the playground.

4. Give children name tags to wear around their neck. Review the names of the ocean vehicles on the name tags. Practice with children by calling the name of each ocean vehicle and asking them to raise their hand when the vehicle they are wearing is called.

How to Play

1. Have each child stand on an *X* around the circle.

2. Explain to children that when you call out the name of one of the ocean vehicles, the children wearing that name tag will change places in the circle with one another.

3. Tell children that when you call out *Stormy weather!*, everyone in the circle changes places.

kayak ○

big ship ○

sub ○

sailboat ○

Provide an opportunity for free play using toy boats and an "ocean" scene.

Materials

- blue plastic tablecloth or a large sheet of blue butcher paper
- colored marking pens
- toy boats of various types

Let's Go Sailing

Preparation

1. Using the blue tablecloth or butcher paper and marking pens, create an ocean with land along the bottom edge and an island in the middle of the water.

2. Collect several small toy boats. Place them in a box when not in use.

How to Play

Allow two or three children at a time access to the activity. Children can use the knowledge they have gained about different types of sea vehicles to act out their own scenarios.

Variation

If you are fortunate enough to have the space and have access to a real boat (small canoe, inflatable boat, paddle boat, etc.), allow children the opportunity to pretend to be sailing, fishing, etc., in the real thing.

Supply items such as slickers, boots, fishing net, fishing pole, binoculars, etc., for children to use along with the boat.

Taking Care of the Ocean

Children learn about the importance
of protecting the ocean and ocean life by
keeping beaches and water free of trash.

Clean It Up!

What a mess!

Let's clean it up!

Dad picked up plastic rings.

Mom picked up bottles.

Tasha picked up cans.

All About the Ocean • EMC 2407 • ©2005 by Evan-Moor Corp.

Jamal and Kim picked up paper.

The beach is clean.
Now they can have a picnic.

What a clean beach!

8

The End

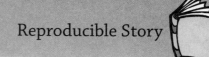

Clean It Up!

What a mess!

1

Let's clean it up!

2

Dad picked up
plastic rings.

3

Mom picked up bottles.

4

Tasha picked up cans.

5

Jamal and Kim
picked up paper.

6

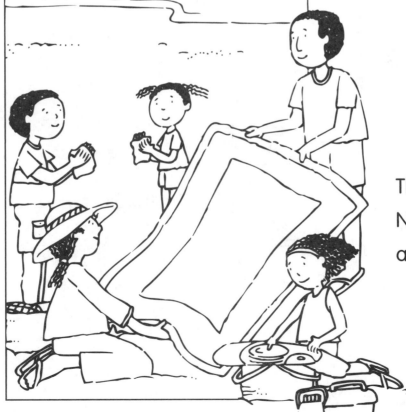

The beach is clean.
Now they can have
a picnic.

7

What a clean beach!

8

The End

Name _____

Cleaning the Beach

Color. Cut. Glue in order.

1	2
3	4

Note: See page 9 for suggestions on using the storyboard pieces on pages 179 and 181 for Clean It Up!

Storyboard Pieces

**Taking Care
of the Ocean**

**Taking Care
of the Ocean**

**Taking Care
of the Ocean**

**Taking
Care of
the Ocean**

**Taking
Care of
the Ocean**

Taking Care of the Ocean

©2005 by Evan-Moor Corp.
All About the Ocean • EMC 2407

Taking Care of the Ocean

©2005 by Evan-Moor Corp.
All About the Ocean • EMC 2407

Taking Care of the Ocean

©2005 by Evan-Moor Corp.
All About the Ocean • EMC 2407

Taking Care of the Ocean

©2005 by Evan-Moor Corp.
All About the Ocean
EMC 2407

Taking Care of the Ocean

©2005 by Evan-Moor Corp.
All About the Ocean • EMC 2407

Taking Care of the Ocean

©2005 by Evan-Moor Corp.
All About the Ocean • EMC 2407

Taking Care of the Ocean

©2005 by Evan-Moor Corp.
All About the Ocean • EMC 2407

Taking Care of the Ocean

©2005 by Evan-Moor Corp.
All About the Ocean • EMC 2407

After making a "clean-up crew" visor, children head out to the playground (or a nearby park) to do some cleaning up. Be sure to set safety parameters such as *Don't touch glass.*

Materials

- page 184, reproduced, one per child
- marking pens or crayons
- scissors
- yarn
- hole punch
- paper bags, one per child

Clean-up Crew

Preparation

1. Reproduce the pattern on page 184 on white construction paper, one for each child.

2. Plan time to model how to decorate and assemble the visor.

3. Remind children of how the family in the story cleaned up the beach. Explain that they are going to clean up the playground (or park) in the same way.

Steps to Follow

1. Children use marking pens or crayons to decorate their visor. Then they cut out the visor.

2. An adult strings yarn through each hole and secures it with a knot.

3. Children put on their visors, take a paper bag, and head for the playground (park) to "clean it up!"

Extension

Have children make posters to remind people to keep the beaches and oceans clean. Write "Keep It Clean!" on white drawing paper. Children add a picture showing someone cleaning up a dirty beach.

Note: Use this pattern with Clean-up Crew art activity.

Visor Pattern

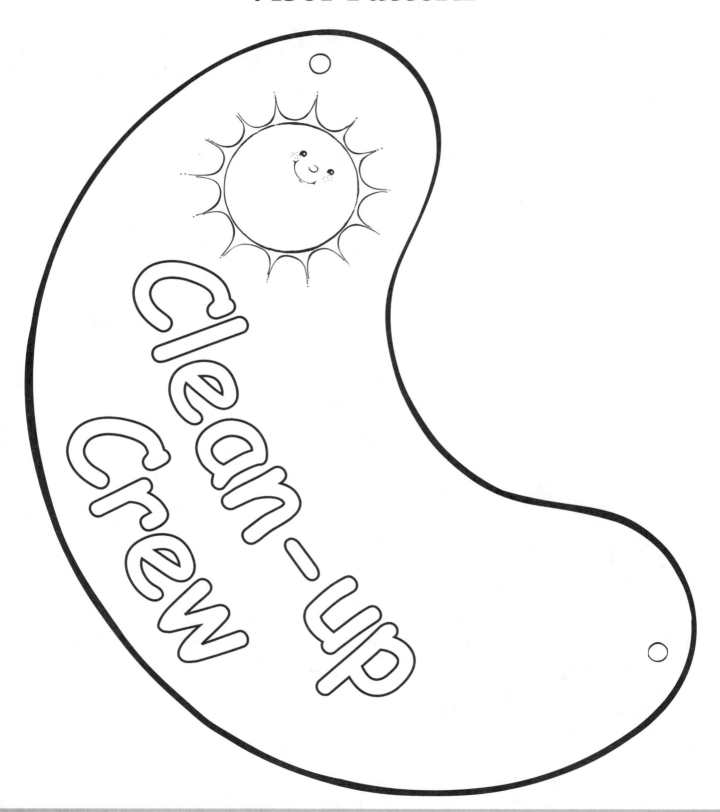

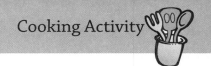

Children use yummy cookie ingredients to create "sand art" in a jar.

Materials

- tag at bottom of page, reproduced, one per child
- quart-sized glass jars or clear plastic jars with a lid, one per child
- measuring cups, several
- measuring spoons, several sets
- yarn
- hole punch
- scissors
- plastic tablecloth

Sand Art Cookies
(fills 1 quart-size jar)

- ½ cup (100 g) sugar
- ½ cup (110 g) brown sugar
- ½ cup (50 g) rolled oats
- ½ cup (50 g) crisp rice cereal
- 1¼ cups (160 g) all-purpose flour
- ½ teaspoon (2–3 g) baking powder
- ½ teaspoon (2–3 g) salt
- ½ cup (86 g) semisweet chocolate chips
- ½ cup (100 g) candy-coated chocolate pieces (M&M's®)

Sand Art Cookie Jars

Preparation

1. Prepare a cooking center with all materials assembled and measured.
2. Cover a table with a plastic tablecloth or butcher paper.
3. Cut out and reproduce the tag at the bottom of this page for each child.

Steps to Follow

1. Children pour each ingredient into their jar, one by one, flattening each ingredient so that it is in a smooth layer.
2. They use a hole punch to make a hole in the tag (assist younger children).
3. Then they cut a piece of yarn, string it through the tag, and tie the tag around the lid of their jar (assist younger children).
4. Children bring their Sand Art Cookie Jar home to bake with their family.

○ # Sand Art Cookies

Preheat oven to 350°F (175°C)

- Empty entire contents of jar into a bowl.
- Add one large egg.
- Add ½ cup of melted margarine. Mix well.
- Form dough into 1" balls.
- Bake on a cookie sheet for 10–12 minutes.

Dear Parent(s) or Guardian(s),

Today we cooked in class. Your child helped prepare a "Sand Art Cookie Jar." Besides having fun, the children practiced:

- vocabulary development
- listening to and following directions
- using small motor skills
- measurement

For our unit *The Ocean,* we will send home a variety of new recipes. Each recipe will be one that your child has tried in class and is excited about. We hope you have an opportunity to bake these delicious cookies with your child. Allowing your child to help in the kitchen is a wonderful way to reinforce learning skills while creating family memories.

Sand Art Cookie Jar

Materials
(fills 1 quart-size jar)

- ½ cup (100 g) sugar
- ½ cup (110 g) brown sugar
- ½ cup (50 g) rolled oats
- ½ cup (50 g) crisp rice cereal
- 1¼ cups (160 g) all-purpose flour
- ½ teaspoon (2–3 g) baking powder
- ½ teaspoon (2–3 g) salt
- ½ cup (86 g) semisweet chocolate chips
- ½ cup (100 g) candy-coated chocolate pieces (M&M's®)

Steps to Follow

1. Pour each ingredient into the jar, one by one, flattening each ingredient so that it is in a smooth layer.

2. Cut out a tag, and use a hole punch to make a hole in the tag.

3. Cut a piece of yarn, string it through the tag, and tie the tag to the lid of the jar.

4. You may give the Sand Art Cookie Jar as a gift, or bake the cookies for yourselves.

Instructions for Preparing Cookies
Preheat oven to 350ºF (175ºC)

- Empty entire contents of jar into a bowl.
- Add one large egg.
- Add ½ cup of melted margarine. Mix well.
- Form dough into 1" balls.
- Bake on a cookie sheet for 10–12 minutes.

Note: After naming all of the items on the page, children decide if the picture belongs on the beach or in the garbage can. Then children color, cut out, and glue the pictures into the correct category.

Language—Categorization

Name _____

On the Beach

Color. Cut. Glue.

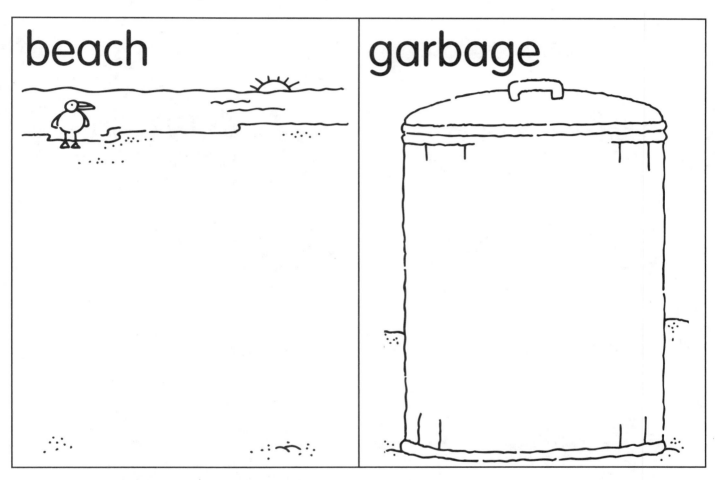

beach

garbage

Note: Children count the cans that remain and then write the answer in each box. You may wish to solve the first problem as a class.

Name _____

Clean the Beach

How many are left? Count. Write the number.

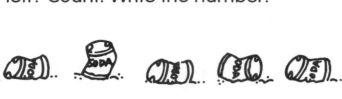

How many are left? | 3 |

How many are left? | |

How many are left? | |

How many are left? | |

Note: Children add the cans together and write the sum in each box.

Name _____

One More

Count the cans. Add. Write the number.

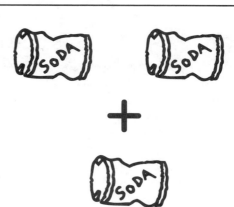

How many? $\boxed{2}$

How many? $\boxed{}$

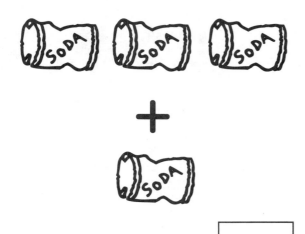

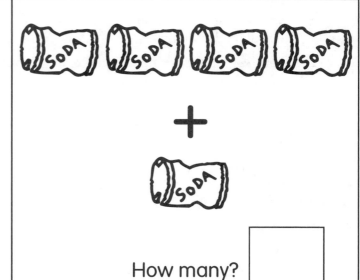

How many? $\boxed{}$

How many? $\boxed{}$

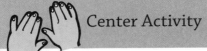

Children clean up the beach! They sort garbage and recyclable garbage into the correct bins.

"Clean It Up!" Sorting Center

Preparation

1. Pour sand into a medium to large tub or bin. This will be the "beach."

2. Label the garbage can and a plastic recycle bin accordingly.

3. Place beach items and trash on the "beach." Set the garbage can and plastic bin at one end of the beach.

4. Plan time to model how the center is used.

Steps to Follow

1. Children work individually or in pairs to clean up the beach.

2. They determine which items are trash and place them in the appropriate receptacle.

3. Children then determine which items belong on the beach and leave them there.

Materials

- medium- to large-size bin or tub

- sand

- small garbage can (labeled "garbage")

- plastic bin (labeled "recycle")

- items found at the beach (shells, driftwood, etc.)

- trash found at the beach (plastic rings, soda cans, food wrappers, etc.)

Note: Sing this song to the tune of "The Mulberry Bush."

Music/Dramatic Play Activity

Teach the children to sing the following words as they pretend to clean up the beach. Use this opportunity for children to wear their "clean-up crew" visors (page 183).

This Is the Way We Clean the Beach

This is the way we clean the beach,
        clean the beach, clean the beach.
This is the way we clean the beach
all through the day.

Verse 2

This is the way we look for trash,…

Verse 3

This is the way we pick up trash,…

Verse 4

This is the way we dump the trash,…

Alphabet Cards

Use these colorful Alphabet Cards in a variety of ways. Simply laminate and cut apart the cards and store them in a sturdy envelope or box.

Alphabet cards can be used to practice skills such as:

- letter recognition
- letter-sound association
- visual perception

Alphabet Card Games

What's My Name?   Use the alphabet cards to introduce the names of the letters, both uppercase and lowercase.

Make a Match   Children match a lowercase and uppercase letter. They then turn the cards over to self-check. If a correct match has been made, the child will see a picture of the same object whose name begins with the letter being matched.

First-Sound Game   Use the alphabet cards as phonics flash cards and ask children to identify the sound of each letter.

ABC Order   Children take all of the uppercase or lowercase cards and place them in alphabetical order.

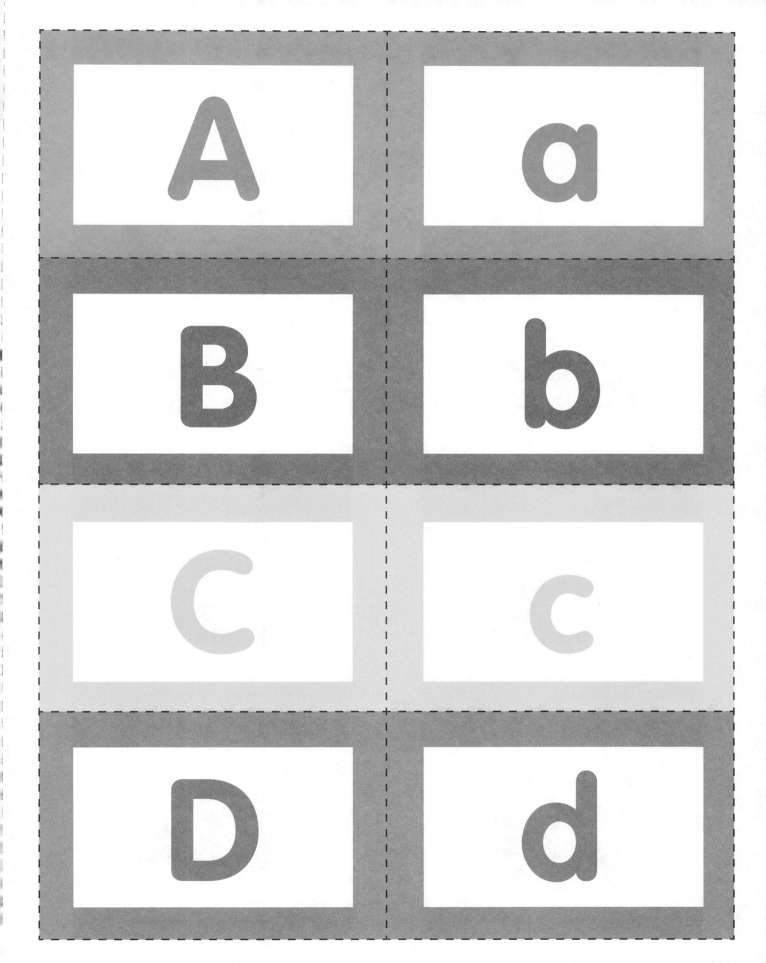

A a

B b

C c

D d

anemone

Anemone

beach

Beach

crab

Crab

dolphin

Dolphin

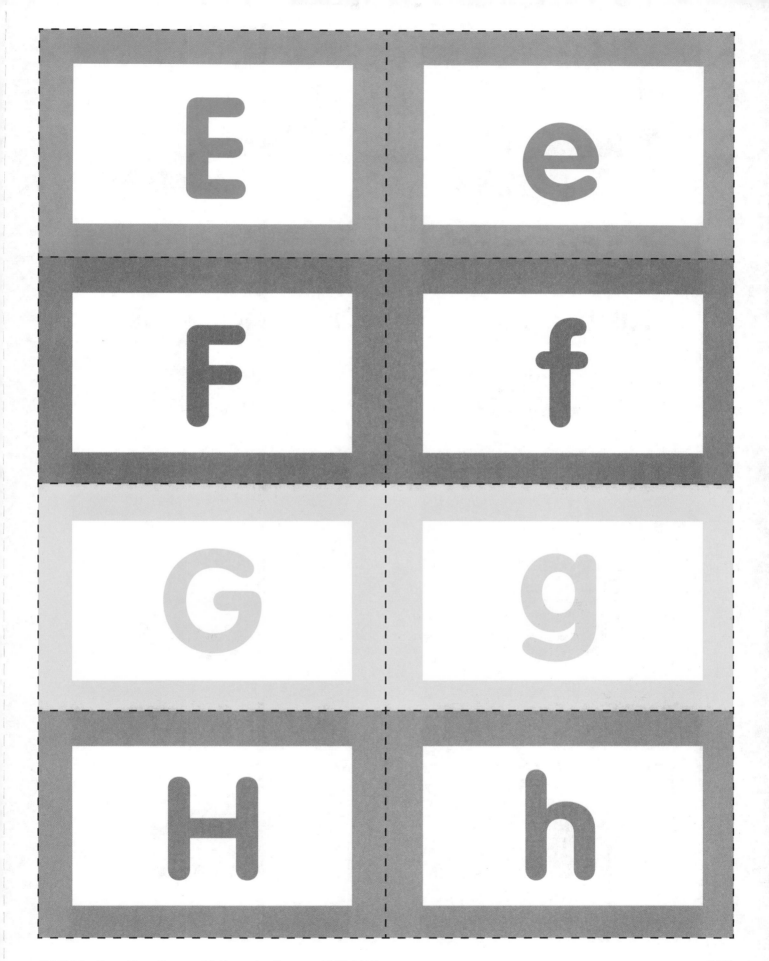

eel

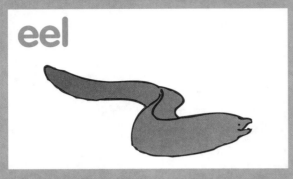

Eel

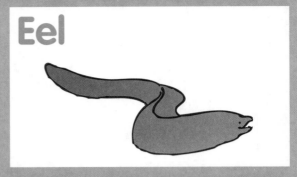

fishing boat

Fishing boat

goldfish

Goldfish

hermit crab

Hermit crab

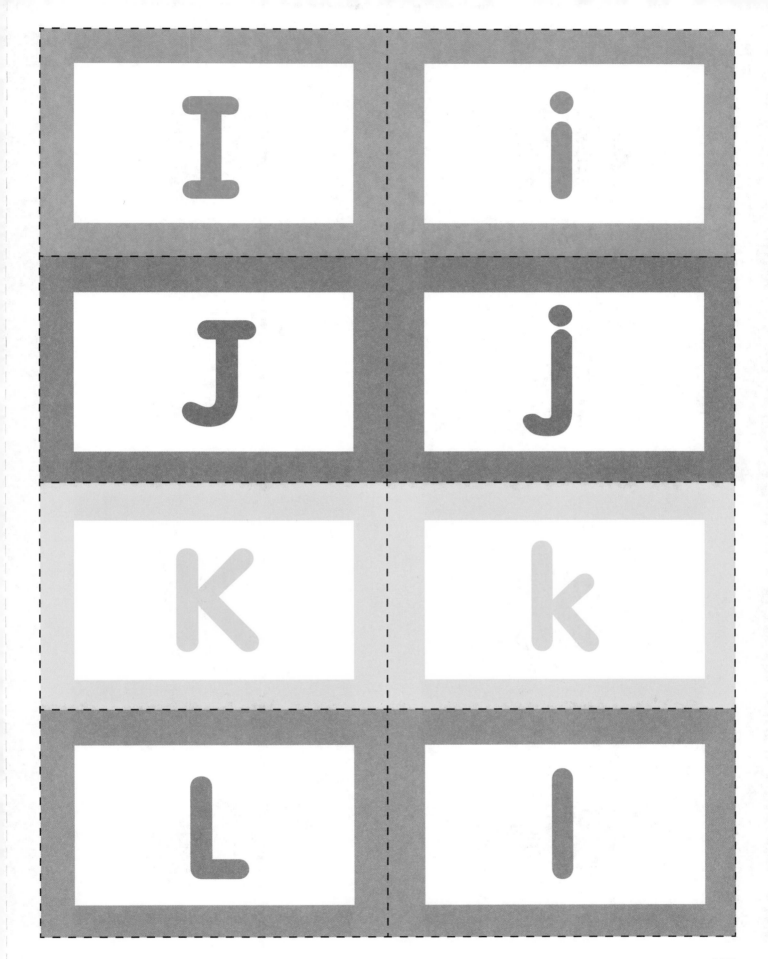

I   i

J   j

K   k

L   l

in

In

jellyfish

Jellyfish

kelp

Kelp

lobster

Lobster

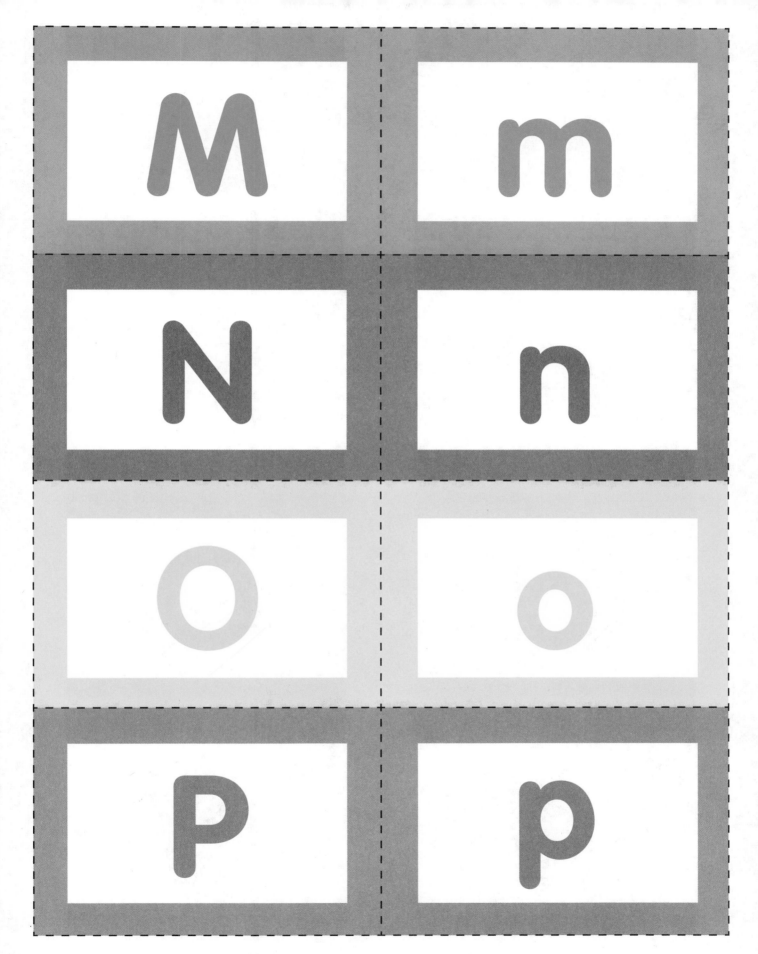

moon

Moon

net

Net

octopus

Octopus

pail

Pail

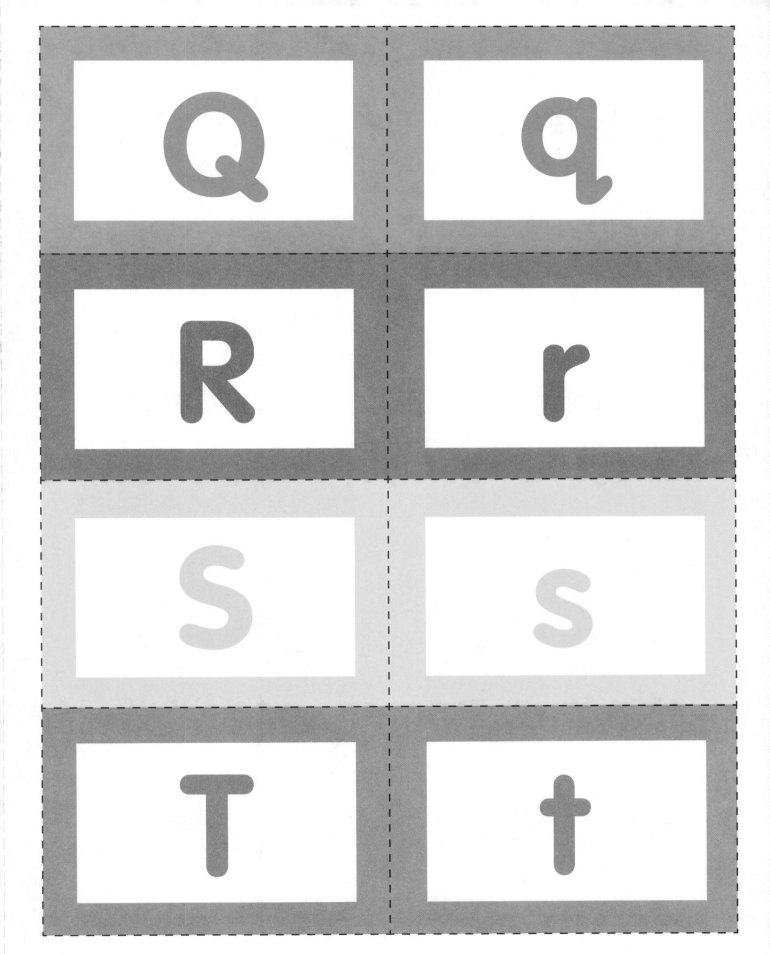

Q q

R r

S s

T t

quiet shh...

Quiet shh...

ray

Ray

submarine

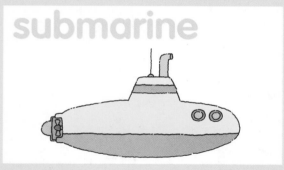

Submarine

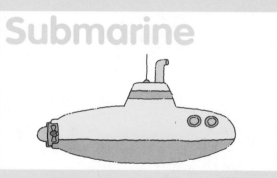

tuna

Tuna

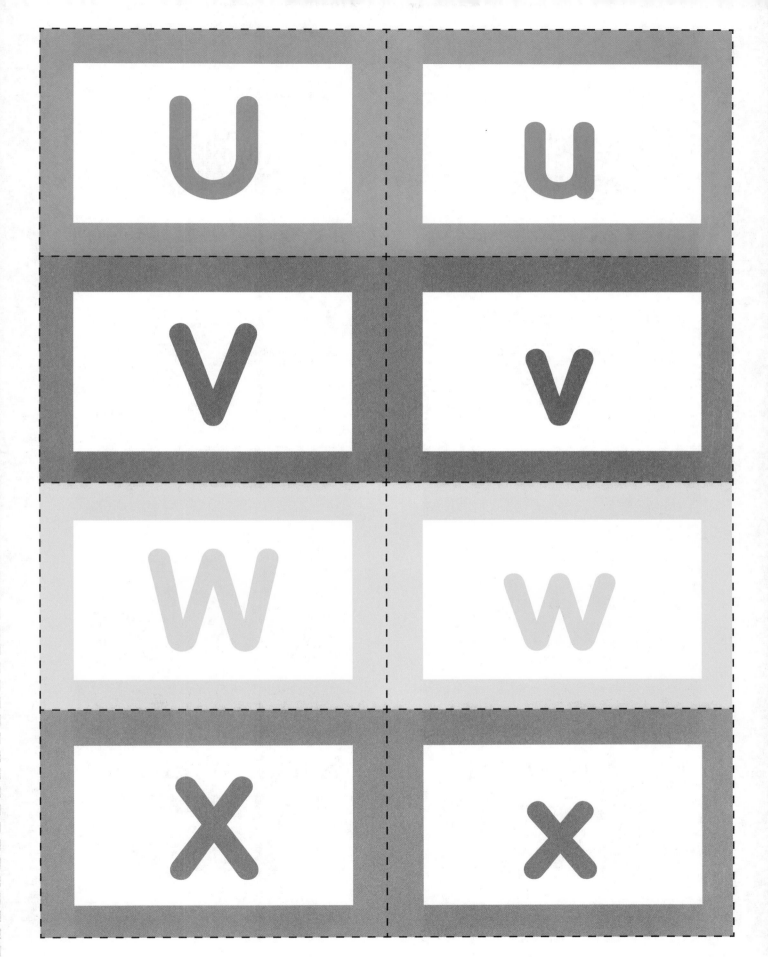

urchin

Urchin

v in the sand

V in the sand

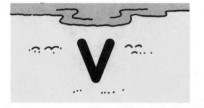

water

Water

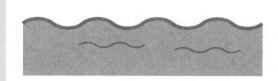

x in the sand

X in the sand

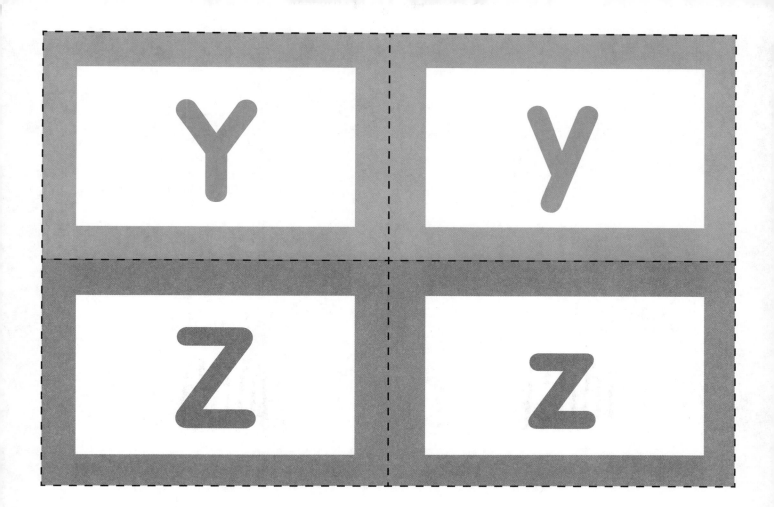

yellow

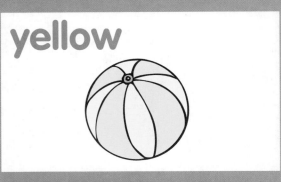

Yellow

zebra fish

Zebra fish

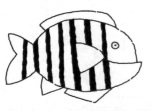

Answer Key

Page 28

Page 39

Page 40

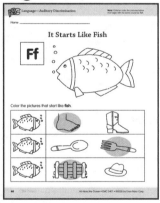

Page 41

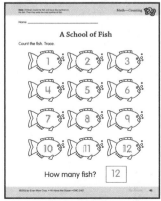

Page 66

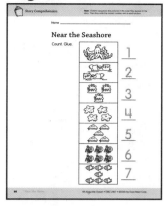

Page 75

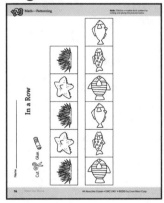

Page 76

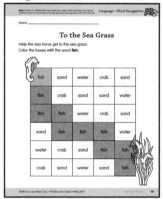

Page 77

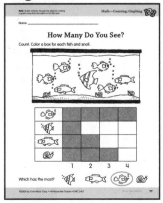

Page 102

Page 114

Page 115

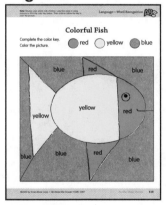

Page 116

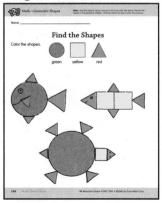

Page 117

Page 158

Page 187

Page 144

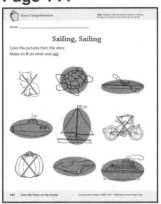

Page 159

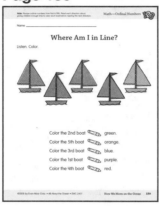

Page 188

Page 157

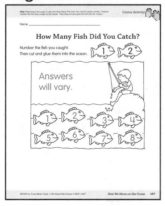

Page 178

Page 189

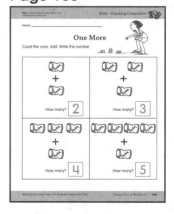